STREET NAMES OF THE CITY OF LIVERPOOL

-REVISED AND UPDATED EDITION-

BY

STEVEN HORTON

COUNTYVISE LTD

First Published 2011 by Countyvise Limited,
14 Appin Road, Birkenhead, Wirral CH41 9HH.

British Library Cataloguing in Publication Data.
A catalogue record for this book is available from the British Library.

ISBN 978-1-906823-57-3

This book is dedicated to Lynne and Luke.
Thank you for supporting me.

CONTENTS

-FOREWORD-
THE WONDERFUL WORLD OF
STREET NAMES

L IVERPOOL HAS A RICH AND COLOURFUL HISTORY, that's second to none! Our heritage therefore, befits any other city throughout the World. The people of Liverpool do take pride in our wonderful heritage, and in particular buildings, so much so, they actually brag about them. Liverpool's array of fine buildings from Georgian to Art-deco has benefited the city to what it is today to boost tourism.

However, buildings stand on streets, and people often wonder how the Streets derive their names! *Street Names of the City of Liverpool* is 'Heaven' sent for people who are inquisitive about Street names. From the most famous Street names to the most ambiguous and the most bizarre names!

From King John's 1207 Royal Charter, Liverpool had Seven Original Streets. The origins of the streets were based on an old Roman Grid Plan. Which in turn, the streets became the epicentre of the town's business fortunes during the early part of Liverpool's prominent rise through trade! I quite often mention Castle Street, and some people are shocked when I tell them it's named after the castle (1235-1723) that stood at the foot of the street. The site of the castle now houses F M Simpson's Queen Victoria Monument.

During the centuries, Liverpool grew in size and a swelling population to match. More and more streets were being laid out to accommodate the new intake of migrants from all over the country and indeed Europe. Street names became vital for the logistics of the city's population. As the city expanded, the more affluent people started to move out into the more leafy suburbs. This movement meant that the city dwellers were now, the working-classes, who were confined to living in extremely small areas.

An example of this is in the Everton area during the 17th and 18th Centuries. Everton Road was a very affluent place to live, where mansions and villas were much sought after! Thomas Rickman's 1814 St. George's Church (the first cast iron building in the world), was Everton's leading landmark. The great English author Thomas De Quincey lived in Everton. Charles Dickens was a regular visitor to the area. However, as the working classes started to encroach into the area, the rich started to move out! Everton during the latter part of the 19th Century and into the 20th Century, therefore, became an 'overspill' for migrants! These migrants were predominately poor Irish and Italian families! The Italians who arrived in Liverpool, made their way to an area in Everton, that became known as 'Little Italy'. This might sound exotic, but it wasn't, it was a slum of back-to-back terraces and courts.

The author, Steve Horton, has done some remarkable in-depth research, that makes a superb historically based Street named book! The book just doesn't give the reader the name of the Street, it also gives the historical significance of why it was named in the first place! This book is a must for all people who love the history of our city! I strongly recommend it, not only as an in-depth guide to Liverpool street names, but also a guide through our history!

Frank Carlyle
(Broadcaster and Historian)

THE ORIGINAL SEVEN STREETS OF LIVERPOOL

ROM THE TIME OF KING JOHN'S CHARTER in 1207 until 1650, Liverpool's layout remained essentially the same. Seven streets formed the built up area of the town and these all remain in existence today in more or less their original position, taking their names from local buildings and features.

During this period, Liverpool's skyline was dominated by the castle, which stood on the site of the present Queen Victoria Monument. This was built in the 13th century on what was high-level rock to the west of the Pool, which was a water inlet that ran along the line of present day Paradise Street and Whitechapel. **Castle Street** connected the castle to the built up area of the town.

Juggler Street, now called High Street, was probably named after the itinerant jugglers that roamed the country practising their art in the centre of towns. The name changed to **High Street** in the early 18th Century, the name traditionally given to the main trading street of a town. However, the change could also have reflected the fact that the construction of the second Town Hall, which had been completed in 1676, had necessitated the removal of the town's High Cross, a feature of towns where people could meet for religious or trading purposes. With Exchange Flags not then in existence, High Street was much longer than its present form as it connected Castle Street with **Old Hall Street**. This led to the Old Hall, which was built in the 13th century by the Moores family as More Hall. They moved to Bank Hall in Kirkdale in the late 14th century and Old Hall, as it became known, was used as a Dower House, where the widow of a deceased male family member would live. This remained a private road until the hall and surrounding lands were sold to the Earls of Derby in 1712, with many wealthy merchants then building properties there.

The three streets mentioned so far all run in a north to south direction, but leading eastwards and eventually out of town were **Dale Street** and **Tithebarn Street**. The former led to a dale and was no more than a rough track in those days that connected with the Townsend Bridge, which crossed the Pool around where the flyovers are now. Tithebarn Street was initially known as Moor Street, as in a heath, rather than in relation to the Moore family who were influential in Liverpool at the time. Around 1524, a tithe barn was erected here, although for some time the street was known by both names. A tithe barn was a building that was used to store a tax of the time known as a tithe, whereby a tenth of produce had to be paid to the clergy. Following the Dissolution of the Monasteries by Henry VIII in 1536 it was owned by Lord Molyneux and used as an ordinary barn.

The final two streets connected the town with the banks of the River Mersey. **Chapel Street** led to the Chapel of St Mary Del Key. This stood on a waterfront site next to the present Church of Our Lady of St. Nicholas and was a chapel of ease to St Mary's, Walton, which was Liverpool's main parish church. After Liverpool became a parish in its own right in 1699, the chapel fell in to disuse and was used as a school and a tavern before it was demolished in 1814. Until the 16th century **Water Street** had been known as Bank or Banke Street as it led to the riverbank in the days before a sea wall was built. This was the main approach to the town for anyone who may have arrived by boat.

LIVERPOOL'S LOST VILLAGES

As LITTLE AS 200 YEARS AGO, what was considered to be Liverpool amounted to the city centre and not much more, with what are now inner city areas being villages in their own right. Although now swallowed up by the expansion of the city, there are many districts of Liverpool where origins of their idyllic village status are evidenced in the street names.

Bevington Bush and **Bevington Street**, separated by the Kingsway tunnel entrance in Vauxhall recall the hamlet of Bevington Bush, situated here in the middle of the 18th century and a popular afternoon stroll for city dwellers. An inn called the Bush was a popular pace to stop for a drink and has spawned the phrase 'going for a bevy'. The idyllic nature of the area is also demonstrated by the small terraced street of **Summer Seat**.

In Anfield, **Sleepers Hill** has been named in relation to two pieces of common land called Great and Little Sleeper. In the middle of the 18th century this formed part of a longer lane that led to West Derby Road and was called Rake Lane. Next to Anfield, the village of Everton was centred around **Village Street**, which now contains no buildings but forms a road the entrance to Everton Park. **Beacon Lane** led to a beacon that stood on the site of St George's Church until it collapsed following a storm in 1803. The beacon, which had been there 500 years, was one of a network around the country on which fires were lit to signify an emergency, such as the Spanish Armada.

In Wavertee village, Wavertree Lake was filled in in 1929 as it was considered too dangerous. This allowed Mill Lane to be widened and is the reason why **Lake Road** was so named. **Monkswell Drive**, **Edgewell Drive**, **Millstead Road** and **Wellstead Road** are named in relation to the Monk's Well which stands at the corner of North Drive and Mill Lane and is reputed to be over 600 years old. Wavertree Mill stood in what is now Beverley Road before it was demolished in 1916, with **Mill Lane** having formed part of the road leading to it. Wavertree's previous importance is also shown by the fact it has an old town hall, **High Street** and was also able to raise taxes, hence **Tithebarn Grove**. **Mosspits Lane** derives from the nature of the land before it was built upon. Like Wavertree, Woolton has a **High Street**, while **Out Lane** was the road out of the village.

Childwall, incorporated into Liverpool in 1913, was referred to in the Domesday Book in 1086 as Cileuuelle, meaning a stream where youngsters meet. The stream in question led from a well near **Well Lane**, to Childwall Brook. The well dried up in the middle of the 18th century and has since been filled in and covered over. **Score Lane** demonstrates the rural nature of Childwall, score meaning pasture. The Childwall Cross, which has given rise to **Crossways**, was erected in its current site in 1935. It had previously lain in a field and may now be nearly 700 years old. **Childwall Abbey Road** leads to the Childwall Abbey Hotel, although there has never been an abbey in Childwall. Research has shown a chapel may have stood on the site in the 15th century however. **Childwall Priory Road** led to Childwall Priory Farm, which was demolished in the 1930s to make way for Queens Drive and the Five Ways roundabout. The farm is said to have stood there for as long as 500 years and the priory may have come from the fact one of the walls of the farmhouse was in the style of a church.

The township of Walton, referred to as Waleton in the Domesday Book, became part of Liverpool in 1895. The area around **Walton Village** contains some of its oldest buildings and **Moor Lane** and **Cherry Lane** are associated with its rural origins.

The importance of West Derby at the time of the Domesday Book is demonstrated by its status as the main centre of the West Derby hundred, an ancient term for a local administrative district. It ruled over Liverpool and other parts of south west Lancashire and had its own castle, leading to today's **Castlefield Road** and **Castlesite Road**. Despite having not been there for several hundred years the footprint of the castle could still be seen as recently as the 1930s when aerial photographs showed the grass being a different shade where it had stood.

Garston became part of Liverpool in 1902. **Island Road** and **Island Road South** and **Holly Farm Road** remember old farms, while **Horrocks Avenue** is named after arguably Liverpool's earliest celebrity. Astronomer Jeremiah Horrocks was born in Otterspool in 1618 and in 1639 predicted and recorded the transit of Venus across the Sun, enabling him to roughly calculate the distance from the Earth to the Sun. He died unexpectedly in 1641 in Toxteth Park and may well have become as famous as Galileo if he had lived for longer.

In the 18th century Old Swan was an important junction, with stagecoaches to Prescot and Wigan continuing down **Prescot Road** and those going to Warrington heading up Broadgreen Road. Black Horse was a hamlet on its own right, consisting of an inn, cottages and blacksmiths and its name lives on today with **Black Horse Lane**, after an inn that stood on the site of the current pub. It was originally Black Moss Lane, referring to one of the many bogs in the vicinity.

THE MOORE AND CROSSE FAMILIES
-LIVERPOOL'S FIRST MERCHANTS-

I N THE LATE 1600s Edward Moore, owner of the Old Hall was the first to extensively develop Liverpool beyond the original streets. Edward was the son of John Moore, a Parliamentarian who was involved in condemning Charles I to death at the end of the Civil War in 1649 and was the earliest known Liverpool man to trade with the West Indies. Edward carried on this tradition and erected a house off Dale Street in the 1660s for the drying and boiling of sugar, which he imported from Barbados. For centuries, his family had owned most of the land between Castle Street, Old Hall Street and the River Mersey and Edward began the process of developing this, with many of the newly built streets remaining in existence today.

Moore Street, linking the castle and river was laid out and named by Edward after himself and still in existence today in a shorter form. Adjoining this is **Fenwick Street**, which is named after his wife, Dorothy Fenwick. Dorothy was a Royalist, a factor which is likely to have saved Edward from having his assets confiscated on the restoration of King Charles II in 1661 as he set out to avenge the death of his father. Another street was laid out at Edward's suggestion along a small piece of farmland between Dale Street and Tithebarn Street owned by John Hackins. This became known as **Hackins Hey**, Hey being a derivation of the French word 'haie', meaning land enclosed by hedges. Hey thus became a common term used in Liverpool to describe small lanes such as this one and **Lancelot's Hey**, which has now been virtually swamped by The Capital (former Royal/Sun Alliance) office building, remembers Thomas Lancelot, a tenant of the Moore family. Related to the Moores were the Hockenhalls of Tranmere. One member, Thomas, was a 17th century mayor of Liverpool and they gave their name to **Hockenhall Alley**, off Dale Street.

Edward later became alarmed by erosion of some of his land and the subsequent loss of rent revenue, so suggested a sea wall to arrest this problem. This went on to be built by his son, Cleave Moore and was named **New Quay**. Cleave Moore did not share his father's passion for foreign trade however and went on to lose a lot of the family estates, selling many to the Stanley's, who were Earls of Derby. In the early 1700s, he did develop some streets off Old Hall Street, some of which were named after his family and are still there. **Edmund Street** was laid out to celebrate his marriage and named after his father in law, Joseph Edmund. **Union Street** formed a cross roads with this and Old Hall Street and may also have been named after the marriage union, although there is no conclusive evidence of this. There is a possibility it may have been to honour the 1707 Act of Union, which joined together England and Scotland, but due to its proximity to Edmund Street I would suggest that the Moore's marriage influence is more likely.

As well as naming streets after members of their family, some of their tenants were commemorated as well. William Bushell rented land near Castle Street on which he had a rope making business and the street where this stood is now called **Old Ropery**. A shipwright called Roger James, a tenant of the family who lived in Moor Street, may have given his name to **James Street**, although there is no evidence to suggest this. He was one of the few people that Edward Moore spoke well of however.

To the north of Liverpool city centre, **Bankhall Lane** once led to Bank Hall, which became the Moores' principal family residence in the 14th century. Bank Hall remained a home of the Moores family for 400 years before being sold to the Earl of Derby. It was eventually demolished in 1772 and a farmhouse built on the site. **Bankhall Street** also takes its name from this.

Along with the Moores, the Crosse family were major landholders in 17th century Liverpool. The family were involved in one of Liverpool's first ventures into overseas trade when Christopher Crosse began importing Spanish iron from Bilbao in the 16th century. The family lived in Crosse Hall, which stood on the site of the present Municipal buildings in Dale Street. Centuries old, this was demolished in 1750 to make way for courts – slum properties consisting of a central courtyard surrounded by two to four storey dwellings on all four sides, giving its name to the adjoining **Crosshall Street**. When the Blue Coat School vacated it old premises due to their limited size and moved to the Blue Coat Chambers in 1717, John Crosse formed a grammar school on the old site. The road leading to this then became known as **School Lane**. In the early 1800s a new road was built to link Tithebarn Street to Byrom Street and Scotland Road. It was named **Great Crosshall Street** after an ancient windmill belonging to the family that stood near to its junction with Johnson Street, the prefix being added to avoid any confusion with Crosshall Street.

THE EARLS OF DERBY & SEFTON

URING LIVERPOOL'S DEVELOPMENT two families, the Stanleys of Knowsley Hall and Molyneuxs of Croxteth Hall were major landowners in the area and their influence can be seen in the names of streets across the city.

The Stanley's have been influential in the Liverpool area since marrying into the Lathom family of Lathom Hall, near Ormskirk, in the 14th century. After Henry VII became King of England following the Battle of Bosworth in 1485, their support was rewarded with the title earls of Derby.

In the English Civil War, the 7th Earl was executed for his support of the King and Lathom Hall was destroyed and their lands confiscated. After regaining their lands following the restoration of the monarchy, Knowsley Hall, once a hunting lodge of the Lathom estate, was developed into the main residence from the early 18th century. A combination of marriages and purchases saw them go on to become major landowners in the Liverpool area.

The 14th earl, Edward Geoffrey Stanley, was Prime Minister three times between 1852 and 1868, while his son Edward served him as Foreign Secretary in his final term. Edward later served Gladstone as Colonial Secretary before going on to lead the Liberals in the House of Lords. The family is still going strong and the current Earl is Edward Stanley. The family's history and influence locally can be seen in the number of streets named after them across the city.

After buying land from Cleave Moore in the early 18th century the Stanleys laid out **Stanley Street** in the city centre around 1740. They also formed **Derby Square** on the site of Liverpool Castle, which remained undeveloped until the 1760s despite being levelled and having its ditch filled in some forty years earlier. Before these streets were built however, the family did have a presence in the town for many centuries through their ownership of Liverpool Tower, their seaside residence at the bottom of Water Street. This would also be used as a stopping off point on their visits to the Isle of Man in their capacity as Lords of Man. The Tower has been gone since c.1821, having been used as a gaol, school and tavern, but its name is remembered by **Tower Garden**, which ran to the east of it.

In the 19th century, some 150 years after lands around Bank Hall were acquired from the Moores, the Stanleys laid out two major roads linking Liverpool and Bootle, where they also owned land. These were **Derby Road** and **Stanley Road**, both developed in the mid 19th century, with a **Stanley Close** being just off the latter. As well as this Rake Lane, which adjoined Stanley Road, was re-named **Latham Street**. **William Moult Street** was also developed, named after one of the family's land agents in the area while **Wilbraham Street** honours Emma Wilbraham, wife of the 14th Earl, who he married in 1824. In Everton, a steward of the Earls gave his name to **Carver Street**, where he had a house.

The Stanley family didn't just buy land in the 19th century, they sold it as well. A large part of the 95 acres of land that became Stanley Park was purchased from them by Liverpool Corporation. Roads near to this that were named in their honour were **Stanley Park Avenue North** and **Stanley Park Avenue South**. The latter was initially plain Stanley Park Avenue but the suffixes were added in the 1930s when Stanley Park Avenue North was developed.

All the streets mentioned so far are in the city centre or north end of Liverpool, but southern areas are not neglected by the Stanley name. Off Prescot Road there is a **Stanley Street**, situated in a district of the same name, while further south there is a **Stanley Street** in Garston and until recent redevelopment there was also a Derby Street. In nearby Grassendale, **Knowsley Road** is named after Knowsley Hall.

The Molyneux family were major landowners in Liverpool from the times of the Plantaganet Kings, who ruled England between 1154 and 1485, when Richard III was killed at the Battle of Bosworth and the Tudors took over the monarchy. In 1446 Henry VI granted Richard Molyneux Croxteth and Toxteth Parks, with Croxteth Hall being built as the family's main residence in 1575. One of the reasons why the family was so well thought of by the royals in this period was the distinction shown by Richard Molyneux in the Battle of Agincourt in 1415, when French troops outnumbered the English by four to one. This is commemorated in West Derby by **Agincourt Road**.

The family were made Earls of Sefton in 1771 but in 1974 Croxteth Hall and Country Park were left to Liverpool City Council after the last Earl had died. Their influence in street names can be seen all over the city, especially in Toxteth and Croxteth.

Between 1446 and 1672 the family were the King's representatives in Liverpool and as such leased the Castle. In the mid to late 17th century **Lord Street** was laid out to connect it with a bridge across the Pool, as on the other side of this was his land at Toxteth Park. This was then mainly rural and used for hunting.

In the late 18th century, as Liverpool became more overcrowded, it was decided to build a new town to the south on the land owned by the Earl of Sefton. Following an Act of Parliament in 1775, building leases could be granted for the land and the boundary between Liverpool and Toxteth Park was re-named **Parliament Street** from its original name of Towns End Lane. The town was only meant to extend as far as Northumberland Street and many of these earliest streets, which were laid out in a grid pattern, were named in honour of the Molyneux family.

The original idea was to call the new town Harrington, but the new name never really caught on and the area continued to be known as Toxteth. The intended name was in honour of Isabella, 1st Countess of Sefton, who was daughter of the Earl of Harrington. However, she is still commemorated by **Upper Harrington Street**, **Stanhope Street** (named after her family surname) and **Upper Stanhope Street**. A relative of hers, Philip Dormer Stanhope, 4th Earl of Chesterfield is remembered by **Chesterfield Street**. Initially there was a Harrington Street, but this was changed to **Caryl Street** after the absorption of Toxteth into Liverpool to avoid confusion with Harrington Street in the city centre. This new name was after Caryl Molyneux, who was the leader of the Royalist troops that ended Prince Rupert's siege of Liverpool during the Civil War.

The Earl of Sefton was himself remembered in **Sefton Street**, while **Warwick Street** and **Upper Warwick Street** recalls the Plantagenet connection. Edward Plantagenet, the 17th Earl of Warwick and claimant to the throne was executed by the Tudor King Henry VII in 1499 to ensure there was no threat to his own ruling dynasty. A name change in the late 19th century saw Bedford Street become **Beaufort**

Street. This was named after the Duke of Beaufort who acted as guardian to Charles William Molyneux, the first Earl, after he became orphaned at the age of eight in 1756. The Beaufort's seat is Badminton House in Avon, which is remembered in **Badminton Street**. **Berkeley Street** is named in relation to Maria Margarita Craven, who married William Philip Molyneux, the 2nd Earl of Sefton in 1792. She was the daughter of Lady Elizabeth Berkeley.

A street that had been present before the development of Toxteth began was **Lodge Lane**, which led to a shooting lodge of the earls of Sefton. This is now called Park Lodge and still stands at the bottom of **Sefton Park Road**, which was named when Sefton Park was opened in 1872. This was developed on 387 acres of land that were purchased from the Earl of Sefton by Liverpool Corporation. Within Sefton Park, **Croxteth Drive** remembers the family's main residence, while **Lathbury Lane** is named after John Lathbury, who was a land agent for the Earl of Sefton and lived in the mid 19th century at Toxteth Farm, to which the lane once led. Nearby there is also a **Croxteth Road**, which dissects Sefton Park Road, as well as a **Croxteth Grove**.

In other parts of the city, there are a number of streets named Sefton in their honour, such as **Sefton Road** in Walton. The Townsend family leased property from the Molyneux family and gave their name to **Townsend Lane**, which was in existence in 1760, as well as **Townsend Avenue**.

Croxteth Hall Lane has led to their ancestral home for hundreds of years, while features of a country estate are present in some of the roads built in new housing developments nearby, such as **Coachmans Drive**, **Foxwood** and **Huntsman Wood**. These roads were developed around the old north east approach to the hall. **Old Kennel Close** has been developed near to where dog kennels were situated during the second half of the 18th century. The kennels that replaced these are still standing in Croxteth Hall Lane and a listed building. **Craven Lea** takes its name from Craven Wood, which is still there and was named in honour of Lord Sefton's marriage to Maria Craven in 1792. Another house belonging to the family was the New Hall, situated near the junction of Muirhead Avenue and Queens Drive. This was demolished to make way for development in 1926, but gave its name to **New Hall Lane**.

THE SLAVE TRADERS OF LIVERPOOL

L IVERPOOL'S ROLE IN THE SLAVE TRADE during the 18th century cannot be ignored. The triangular trade involved the shipping of Lancashire produced goods such as cloth to Africa, which were traded for slaves. They were then transported to America and traded for sugar and tobacco before the ships returned to Liverpool. Given the diversity of products involved within the trade, it may be that there was no merchant in Liverpool during this period that was not involved in some way. This chapter only intends to deal with those who were linked more prominently than others but the distance between some of the streets concerned demonstrates how many people were involved.

Britain's largest Caribbean colony was Jamaica, where many local merchants had estates. These estates were a major source of sugar and a destination for many slave ships and **Jamaica Street**, near to the docks, was developed in the second half of the 18th century in recognition of this. Around the same time and in the same vicinity **Norfolk Street** was laid out, named after a port in Virginia that played an important part in the shipping of goods from the plantations. **Goree**, which is the northbound carriageway of the main road by the Cunard Buildings, is named after an island off Senegal where slaves would gather for shipment to the plantations. British forces had captured this island from the French in 1759.

One of Liverpool's main shopping streets is **Bold Street**, which is named after a family who owned land at the top of the street, where St. Luke's Church stands today. One member of the family was Jonas Bold, who was listed as an African merchant in 1750. In addition to Bold Street, there is also a **Bold Place** and **Back Bold Street**. Another street linked to slavery in the pedestrian shopping area is **Tarleton Street**, named after the Tarleton family who were slave merchants over three generations from the 1720s. Tom Tarleton, 'The Great T', established the family as leading figures, following in his father's footsteps as a slave merchant. He left a reputed fortune of £80,000 and three of his sons went into partnership with Daniel Backhouse, creating the firm Tarleton and Backhouse. By the 1780s they were reputed to be supplying 3,000 slaves a year to the Spanish colonists. The Tarletons are also responsible for the name of **Redcross Street**, which forms the entrance to a car park at the rear of the Queen Elizabeth II Law Courts. This is named after a red stone obelisk that they erected nearby.

Off Hope Street lies **Blackburne Place**. This was named after John Blackburne, a slave merchant who lived there in the 1780s. Back then, this area was in the country and such a desirable residence could only be afforded by the very wealthy, which he had become from the trade. His house, Blackburne House still stands and is now an education college, exhibition and conference centre. Blackburne was originally from Orford, near Warrington, which he remembered with **Great Orford Street**, off Mount Pleasant. He also engaged in the salt trade and his refinery was situated near to Salthouse Dock, which is situated opposite Canning Place and has given its name to **Salthouse Quay**. In 1798 he moved his salt refinery to Garston, where his name is also remembered in **Blackburne Street**.

One of the streets running between Brownlow Hill and Pembroke Place is **Great Newton Street**, named after John Newton (1725-1807). As Vicar of Olney, he co-wrote the Olney Hymns, of which Amazing Grace is the best known. Despite eventually campaigning for the abolition of the slave trade, he was captain of a slave ship between 1750–4 while studying for the ministry in Liverpool. This ship was called the African and was owned by Joseph Manesty, who was the town's bailiff in 1757 and lived in Manesty's Lane off Hanover Street, which has now been re-aligned and re-named **New Manesty's Lane** as part of the Liverpool One redevelopment. Near the corner of Renshaw Street and Hardman Street is **Oldham Street**, along with **Oldham Place**. These are named after Captain James Oldham, who was engaged in the Africa to West Indies section of the triangle and built the first house in the street. He died at sea in 1825.

Foster Cunliffe, who was mayor three times is commemorated in the city's business district by **Cunliffe Street**. He owned an estate at Chesapeake Bay in Virginia where he sent nearly 2,000 slaves to work. His firm, Foster Cunliffe and Sons owned or had a share in four vessels, which were regularly used for slave trading. Another who transported slaves to Chesapeake was Richard Gildart, who was Mayor in 1714, 1731 and 1736 and lived until the age of 99. He had been associated with transporting Jacobite rebels (supporters of the deposed James II) to America in 1716 and then came to prominence in the slave trade. His son and grandson, both called James, were also Mayors of Liverpool. **Gildart Street**, off London Road, is named in the family's honour, while nearby **Norton Street** takes its name from Norton Hall, a residence of theirs that stood on the street's corner with Islington. The family also gave their name to **Gildarts Gardens** in Vauxhall as they had a summer residence in the area.

In the 1750s John Ashton, who owned the salt works at Dungeon, near Speke (a name derived from the old English word dunge – land next to a marsh) went into the slave trade and in turn invested the profits into the Sankey Canal. His son, Nicholas, purchased Woolton Hall (which still stands today) in 1772 and is remembered in the neighbourhood by **Ashton Square**, as well as **Ashton Drive** in nearby Hunts Cross. The family is also commemorated in the city centre, where there is an **Ashton Street** off Brownlow Hill. Not far from this is **Little Woolton Street**, which was named after the family home.

As well as selling estates to the Stanleys, Cleave Moore sold some of his land around Old Hall Street to the Earle family, who laid out **Earle Street** there. John Earle, an ironmonger served on the Town Council and went into slavery after 1750. His two sons, Ralph and Thomas, both became Mayors and continued the family's involvement in the trade, with Thomas acquiring land outside the city centre known as the Spekelands Estate. This was situated between the current Smithdown Road and Tunnel Road and on it he built a house called Spekelands in 1803, living there until he died in 1822. This land was then built upon around 1870 and **Earle Road** and **Spekelands Road** were named in the family's honour. **Woodcroft Road** was named after a house of the same name that stood on the estate. Carrying on down Smithdown Road one of Liverpool's most famous streets **Penny Lane**, immortalised by the Beatles song, has been said in the last five years to have been named after merchant James Penny. He spoke against abolition at a parliamentary committee set up in 1788 to look at the trade, saying it would cause the city great harm and going as far as saying that the slaves on his ships had ventilation and sufficient space, enabling them to sleep better than the gentlemen ashore. However, there is no evidence to suggest Penny had any land or property in the area and in the 1841 census the road is actually listed as 'Pennies Lane', so I believe the link is more than likely to have been made as it creates a good story rather than on any factual basis.

In the north of the city two different slave traders, John Atherton and Thomas Leyland, had ownership of Walton Hall. Leyland acquired the property, which stood on the site of the boating lake in Walton Hall Park, from Atherton in 1804. Leyland first accumulated his wealth in a lottery win in 1776, but went on to invest it in ships that were used for privateering and slave trading. The hall was demolished in the early 20th century but is still remembered by **Walton Hall Avenue**, which was opened by George V in 1934.

The Slave Trade was finally abolished in 1807, with the last slave ship sailing into the Mersey that year being captained by Hugh 'Mind Your Eye' Crow, who hailed from the Isle of Man. The nickname for him came from the fact he lost an eye in infancy, meaning others would regularly shout 'mind your eye' to him. He would later write his memoirs and died in 1829. **Crow Street**, off Stanhope Street, is named after him.

In 2006 there was a call to wipe Liverpool's slave trading streets from the map altogether. Councillor Barbara Mace called for those named after the most notorious traders to be re-named after people who had done something positive, however the plan was rejected as it was felt the city's history should not simply be airbrushed over.

LIVERPOOL'S SLAVERY ABOLITIONISTS

WHILE MANY MERCHANTS undoubtedly made a healthy living from slavery, this is not to say that Liverpool was not without its abolitionists who did everything they could to have the trade stopped. The Society for the Abolition of the Slave Trade was formed in London in 1787 and soon followed by the Liverpool Committee for the Abolition of the Slave Trade. Slavery was finally outlawed in 1807.

Perhaps the most famous of the local abolitionists was William Roscoe. A self-taught man, he was a lawyer, banker, author and poet, as well as MP for Liverpool. He spoke against the trade in parliament and was known as someone who may bring down the town because of his views. Despite this he was held in great honour and **Roscoe Street** was named after him some 35 years before his death in 1831. Another street named in his honour is **Roscoe Lane**, which links Roscoe Street with Berry Street. He was buried in the grounds of the Renshaw Street Unitarian Chapel which is now a small alternative retail complex, occupied by many of the businesses that left Quiggins in School Lane when it was demolished in 2007. The site of the burial grounds remains however under the name of **Roscoe Memorial Gardens**.

One of Roscoe's homes in the 1780s was a house called the Birchfield, situated at the corner of the present day Islington and Canterbury Street. As this area became more built up, he left for Allerton Hall, but **Birchfield Street** commemorates the house that stood until the end of the 19th century. Another home of Roscoe's was a cottage called Bentley, which is remembered by **Bentley Road** in Toxteth. In 2004 **Garrison Close** was built off Bentley road, named after William Lloyd Garrison (1805-79), who fought for the abolition of slavery in the USA, editing the Liberator magazine and being one of the founders of the American Anti Slavery Society.

One of Roscoe's poems, about a stream in Dingle was named The Nymph of Dingle. This stream has long dried up but its name lives on in **Dingle Vale**. William Roscoe's sister Margaret married Daniel

Daulby from Westmoreland, who owned land adjoining Pembroke Place and cut **Daulby Street** through it. The couple took up residence there after they were wed.

In 1696 William Rathbone II arrived in Liverpool from Gawsworth in Cheshire and established a timber business, which was developed along with an international merchanting concern by his son, William Rathbone III (1726-89). He was a committed opponent of the slave trade as was his son William Rathbone IV (1757-1809), who was a founder member of the abolition movement in Liverpool. The Greenbank Estate near Sefton Park was leased from the Earl of Sefton in 1788 as a country retreat and gives its name to **Greenbank Lane**, **Greenbank Drive** and **Greenbank Road**. Greenbank House still stands within the University of Liverpool site. In Wavertree the family are commemorated by **Rathbone Road** while off this is **Binns Road**, named after Dr. Jonathan Binns (1747-1818), a Liverpool medicine man who was a co-founder of the abolition committee.

THE LONDON INFLUENCE

I N THE 18TH CENTURY, it became fashionable around the country to name streets and districts after areas of London, Piccadilly in Manchester being one example. Liverpool, which was well on its way to becoming a major international city, was no exception to this and a number of old lanes that were developed were renamed after London streets or districts.

London Road was once part of the 'road to Prescot', the main road out of Liverpool. This led all the way to Warrington, but was in such poor condition in the early 18th century that it had to be traversed on horseback. In 1760 it was widened and repaired, meaning that it was now possible to take carriages from Liverpool to all parts of the country, instead of having to pick one up at Warrington. The first coaches from Liverpool to London used to leave from Dale Street and the old road was formally named London Road.

Another route out of Liverpool in the 18th century was Pinfold Lane, which led north towards Bank Hall and Bootle. That was named after a pinfold, a pound for stray animals that was situated near the tithe barn. By 1810 this lane had been renamed **Vauxhall Road**, after a house that was built there and named after Vauxhall Gardens in the London district of Lambeth. They were named after a widow Jane Vaux, although historians disagree who she was actually the widow of, with Guy Fawkes being one argument and the Vaux being a derivation.

One of the earliest lanes of Liverpool was Dig Lane, which connected Tithebarn Street and Dale Street on the outer fringes of town. This was re-named **Cheapside** by 1725, after an area of the City of London that derived from the old English word for market. A new street northwards was **Pall Mall**, which had begun to be developed by 1765 and takes its London origins from a version of croquet that was played in the late 17th century. **Whitechapel** was re-named after the east London district in the 1770s, having originally been called Frogg Lane due to the fact that the area was a breeding ground for frogs. Whitechapel in London was named after the colour of the parish Church of St Mary, which dates from the 13th century.

Liverpool's first purpose built theatre was constructed in 1749, replacing an earlier venue named the Old Ropery that had become unsuitable as it had no boxes or gallery. The new theatre was situated near Water Street and the road fronting it was named **Drury Lane**, after the famous London theatre. It remained in use until 1772 when another one was built in Williamson Square. After this it went into decline and was used as a warehouse and fire engine shed until its demolition under the 1786 Improvement Act that allowed for slum clearance. Drury Lane in London took its name from Sir William Drury, a 16th century statesman and soldier.

Several University of Liverpool buildings are located on **Oxford Street**, although this is not named after the famous Oxford University. This street was laid out at the beginning of the 19th century, nearly 100 years before Liverpool's university was founded. It was named after London's Oxford Street, which was so named as it was the road to Oxford. On the waterfront and initially laid out in the late 18th century as Wapping Quay, **Wapping** takes its name from a district of the London docklands, deriving from an Anglo Saxon name meaning 'Wappa's people'.

The Ranelagh tea gardens stood from 1722-90 on the site of the Adelphi Hotel. This name was copied from gardens in the house of Lord Ranelagh in the London district of Chelsea. **Ranelagh Street**, which led to the Liverpool tea gardens, was in existence by 1766. Also in existence by 1766 was nearby **Fleet Street**, the London version being named after a river of the same name that now flows underground. **Newington**, which runs between Bold Street and Renshaw Street, was developed and in existence by 1785 and is named after a district of south London, literally meaning 'new town'.

The old rural lane leading to West Derby was called Folly Lane, after a building of 6-8 storeys called 'The Folly' that stood near to the Wellington Monument. A fair known as Folly Fair used to take place in the fields adjoining it every Easter, which had a reputation for drunkenness and fighting. Around 1780 the folly had been purchased and a house built on its site by Philip Christian. As local fields were swamped by development at the turn of the 19th century, the new main road was re-named **Islington**. This district of north London was mentioned in the Domesday Book and has Anglo Saxon origins.

Off Islington is **Soho Street**, named after a district of west London that takes its name from a hunting call used to call in the hounds, as it was once a hunting ground attached to Westminster Palace. Two other rural lanes were re-named around the same time as Islington, both after districts of west London. A previously unnamed continuation of Brownlow Hill was named **Paddington**, which in London was named after an Anglo Saxon chief called Padda, while part of the turnpike road to Prescot, Prescot Lane, was re-named **Kensington**. Like Islington, Kensington is also mentioned in the Domesday Book and has Anglo Saxon origins.

MERCHANTS AND MAYORS OF THE 18TH AND EARLY 19TH CENTURIES

D URING THE 18TH CENTURY Liverpool grew at an astounding pace, the population rising several fold. During this time the Town Council consisted mainly of merchants and was self-elected. Once on it, a member would sit for life, with two bailiffs (who enforced municipal orders) and a Mayor being appointed on an annual basis. Many of these merchants and their activities are reflected in the street names in the city centre and hardly a Mayor of Liverpool during this period did not have a street named after him. However many have since disappeared due to redevelopment.

At this time, the area governed by Liverpool's council was much smaller than now. In the north for example, it only stretched as far as **Boundary Street**, which marks the original dividing line between Liverpool and Kirkdale, while nearby there is **Townsend Street**. There is a **Boundary Lane** two miles east of the city centre off West Derby Road, but this didn't mark a boundary with Liverpool, instead that between Everton and West Derby. **Mile End** in Vauxhall marks one mile from the Town Hall.

Some of Liverpool's earliest mayors are commemorated in the area around Dale Street, Tithebarn Street and Old Hall Street. **Fazakerley Street**, for example, was in existence in the early 18th century as Rosemary Lane, but had its name changed by 1785. The Fazakerley family of Walton owned the land here and one member, Roger, was Mayor in 1531, with Samuel Fazakerley later serving as Town Clerk from 1664 to 1668. Off Fazakerley Street, **Spellow Place** commemorates one of their mansions. Two members of the Brooks family, Gilbert and Egidius, were Mayor in 1592 and 1601 respectively. They were from a long established family that is commemorated by **Brook Street**.

Bixteth Street and **Sweeting Street** are named after two mayors from the turn of the 18th century, Alderman Thomas Bickerstath (1701) and Alderman Sweeting (1698). Bixteth Street, where Thomas lived, was laid out in the early 1700s as Bickersteth Street but this was corrupted to Bixteth by 1765, while Sweeting Street was originally known as Elbow Lane due to its shape. Sweeting Street became the first Liverpool street to have a proper sign for it. Opposite Bixteth Street is **Tempest Hey**, which was developed in the early 1700s and named after the Plumbe Tempest family of Plumbe Hall in Wavertree. **Rigby Street** was in existence by 1785 and named after Gilbert Rigby who had been Mayor in 1774 and lived on the street's corner with Old Hall Street. One of the few remaining narrow alleys of Liverpool is **Leather Lane** off Dale Street, where leather skins were sold in the 18th century.

A cockpit, which was a circular pit dug into the ground once existed in what is now **Cockspur Street**. Cock fighting, which originated in ancient Persia, Greece and Rome, was a fairly gruesome form of entertainment for the merchants. The 'sport' was not outlawed in England until 1849

At the Vauxhall Road end of Tithebarn Street is **Pownall Square**. This is named after William Pownall, who was mayor in 1767 but died in office, catching a chill while trying to quell a riot at Devils Acre, near Salthouse Dock. Pownall lived on the corner of Liver Street and **Pownall Street**, which had been named when he was still alive and is situated off Park Lane. This street was originally much longer than it is now, part of it having become **Upper Pownall Street** around 1900. His home village of Tabley in Cheshire was commemorated by **Tabley Street**, which was laid out through land that he owned near his property.

On the opposite side of Park Lane to Pownall Street is **Cleveland Square**, named after John Cleveland who was Mayor in 1703 and later MP between 1710 and 1713. Cleveland owned the land on which **Price Street** was laid, naming it after a branch of his extended family. Nearby there once existed a Bird Street, which was absorbed into Strand Street in the late 18th century. This was named after Alderman Bird, who lived in the street and was Mayor in 1746, but he was not to be forgotten and **New Bird Street**, off Jamaica Street was named in his honour instead.

Blundell Street is named after the Blundell family. Bryan Blundell (1676-1756) had an interest in the slave ship Mulberry, but his main concern was as a tobacco merchant. He was twice mayor of Liverpool and founded the Blue Coat School, an interest his two sons, Richard and Jonathan, retained for forty years after his death. The Blue Coat still exists today in Wavertree, although the old school building remains in use as an art gallery and is the oldest building in Liverpool city centre. Its educational link is reflected by the name of the street it stands on, **College Lane**. This was originally called Workhouse Lane after a workhouse that stood on Hanover Street between 1732 and 1795.

Peter Rainford, who was bailiff in 1724 laid out a market garden which became known as **Rainford Gardens** and **Rainford Square**, both of which were in existence by 1765 and to be found between Lord Street and Stanley Street. Another square laid out was **Williamson Square**, developed as an exclusive neighbourhood in the 1760s by the Williamson family, who were shoemakers that invested in overseas trade. William Williamson was Mayor in 1761 and shortly after Williamson Square was completed, nearby **Williamson Street** was developed. An unnamed road led from Williamson Square to Limekiln Lane (now Lime Street), then on the outskirts of town. This was later named **Roe Street**, after merchant William Roe who lived in Queen Square in a house that became the Stork Hotel, which was not demolished until the 1970s. **Richmond Street**, connecting Whitechapel with Williamson Square, was named after the mayor of 1672, Silvester Richmond.

Before 1750, open countryside surrounded the area that is now **Clayton Square** shopping centre. The leaseholder of the land was Sarah Clayton (1712-79), the daughter of colliery owner William Clayton who was MP from 1698 to 1714 and had been Mayor of Liverpool in 1689. Sarah Clayton laid out a square and the adjoining streets on the land. The square's size was halved in 1922 when the Owen Owen store (now Tesco Metro) was built. Even further development took place in the 1980s when the shopping mall was built but the original name has survived. The surrounding streets laid out by Clayton are all still there, although some have shortened in length over the years due to building work. **Leigh Street** is named after her mother, Elizabeth Leigh, while three other streets are named after the husbands of her sisters. They are **Cases Street**, **Houghton Street** and **Parker Street**.

Henry Trafford, who had played a part in the construction of Liverpool's first dock, was mayor in 1740 but died in office. Trafford's

Weint was named after him and later became Trafford Street, but from the 1820s this was merged with a street called Love Lane to form **South John Street**, an extension of North John Street. Having once been a busy road route and entrance to the Paradise Street bus station, it now exists as a pedestrian part of the Liverpool One development. Nearby is **Dorans Lane**, which links Lord Street and Cavern Walks. This was named after an Irish merchant called Felix Doran who lived in Lord Street.

Near the corner of Hanover Street and School Lane is **Brooks Alley**, which was named after a merchant called Joseph Brooks who owned the garden through which it was laid. On the other side of Hanover Street, George Campbell was a sugar boiler and merchant, who was Mayor in 1763 and owned premises on Duke Street. There he dealt in sugar produced by slaves in the West Indies and **Campbell Street** was named after him. Further up Duke Street, Richard Kent, a merchant and ship owner built himself a house in 1768. He then laid out a street adjoining this and named it **Kent Street**. Other streets were developed in this area and named by him in relation to southern counties like his surname. They are **Suffolk Street** and **Surrey Street**.

Thomas Seel was a merchant who traded in tobacco and rum. He lived in Hanover Street and **Seel Street** was laid out through his gardens at the end of the 18th century. Parallel to this is **Parr Street**, named after a banker called Thomas Parr who lived in **Colquitt Street**, which is named after the Colquitts who owned the land through which it was laid. One of the family members, John was listed in Gores Directory of 1766, an annual directory of notable inhabitants, as the ports customs collector. Seel Street and Parr Street are both long streets that were developed on the site of old ropewalks, which were needed in the town due to Liverpool's status as a port. The rope walk method of rope making meant that areas with long straight sites were needed, as a machine would simply move slowly on rails twisting the fibres into strands of rope. As Liverpool grew rope making moved further afield to Toxteth, off Lodge Lane and this can be seen by the long nature of the streets there, as many fields used for rope making were then converted into streets quite easily. Another example of an old ropewalk in the city centre is **Renshaw Street**, which was named after its 18th century owner, John Renshaw.

It is a common misconception that **Hope Street** is so called as it connects Liverpool's two cathedrals. The street was in fact there for

150 years before building work commenced on the Anglican Cathedral. It was named after William Hope, a merchant who built the first house in the street on the site of the Philharmonic Hotel. Off Hope Street is **Maryland Street**, which was developed by a tobacco merchant named Mr Hunter. He lived in Mount Pleasant and this street, along with **Baltimore Street** and **South Hunter Street** were laid out in the gardens of his home. Maryland and Baltimore Streets were named after the location of the plantations and port from which the goods were shipped, while South Hunter Street was so named as a Hunter Street already existed in the north of the city.

Faulkner Street and **Falkner Square** remember Edward Faulkner, who was a late 18th century merchant and High Sheriff of Lancashire. The differing spellings may have been caused by sign-writers not being aware of the exact spelling. During his time as High Sheriff, he raised 1,000 local men when a French invasion threatened in 1797. The square was initially intended to be called Wellington Square but changed in honour of Faulkner after his death at his son Edward Deane Faulkner's recommendation, due to too many other places having this name already. Faulkner also built Fairfield Hall to the east of the town, which gave its name to the surrounding district and subsequently **Fairfield Street** and after his death in 1827 Edward Deane Faulkner, developed the estate further, leading to the naming of **Deane Road**.

The merchants of Liverpool needed somewhere known as an exchange to conduct their business as their quarters at the top of Castle Street became too congested. In 1808 an area adjacent to the current Town Hall was purposely developed and named **Exchange Flags**, its name coming from the flagstones that covered the square. **Exchange Passage East** and **Exchange Passage West** were developed as alleys to connect it with the main street networks, while **Exchange Street East** is named due to its position running adjacent to the previous exchange. Merchants also had to pay duties on imported goods and a new Custom House was built next to the Old Dock in 1722, replacing the one that had stood at the bottom of Water Street. Custom House Lane led to the new building, which was later replaced by a much grander effort that was destroyed by bombing during the Second World War. Custom House Lane itself has now disappeared to make way for the John Lewis store, but **Custom House Place**, running alongside it keeps the memory alive.

Two men who owned land between Brownlow Hill and Pembroke Place around 1800 who had streets named after them were a Mr Dansey and Mr Gill, who give their names to **Dansie Street** and **Gill Street**. These streets are near to **Brownlow Hill** and **Brownlow Street**, which are named after Lawrence Brownlow who also owned a lot of land in this vicinity. Also running uphill from Lime Street is **Copperas Hill**, which is named after some copperas works that were owned by Richard Hughes, Mayor in 1756. Copperas is an old name for ferrous sulphate, which was used in the manufacture of old inks. Liverpool had a thriving pottery industry in the 18th century and one potter who built a house on the corner of **Christian Street** and Islington was Philip Christian.

A civic leader who is not remembered by his surname is Pudsey Dawson, a merchant and ship owner who was mayor in 1799. He regularly used to give talks at the Athenaeum Club when taking snuff and is remembered by his first name in **Pudsey Street**, as Dawson Street was already in existence. Linking Pudsey Street to Lime Street is **Coal Street**, which was the site of a market for Prescot Coal. **Lime Street** takes its name from limekilns that once stood on the site of Lime Street station. It had been known as Limekiln Lane in the mid 18th century but due to the expanding population the kilns were moved around the turn of the 19th century to the North Shore, where Princes and Waterloo Docks are today. A proprietor of the North Shore limekilns was commemorated in **Chadwick Street**, while in Vauxhall **Limekiln Lane** was named after limekilns were established there. Prior to the onset of limekilns and expansion of the dock system, this area had been a popular bathing resort. A popular inn was owned by a Dutchman named Vandries, who gave his name to **Vandries Street**, while **Bath Street** was named after the seawater baths that had to make way for the construction of Princes Dock in 1817. One of the new businesses that developed in the area as the docks developed was the oil crushing works of Earles and Carter, which gave rise to **Oil Street**. Also in this group of streets is **Porter Street**, after Thomas Colley Porter who was mayor in 1827.

With so much development in Liverpool going on at this time, building workers were at a premium and there were profits to be made. In late 18th century two brothers named Johnson came to Liverpool and set up a building business, naming the street on which it was developed **Johnson Street**, where they also owned adjoining land. They later purchased some more land to build some lime works and named this **Hatton Garden**, after their home village, which is near Warrington. Near to these streets is **Pickop Street**, which was named after the Miles and Pickop brewery that existed there 200 years ago. Responsible for the repair of Liverpool's streets at this time was George Byrom, a builder and pavior who had his yard in Hunter Street. **Byrom Street** takes its name from him, although it was originally known as Dog Kennel Lane as it used to house the Corporation pack of hounds that was used for hunting.

Towards the end of the 18th century, merchants began to move away from the central area as it became more crowded with court property. A popular location was the slopes leading towards Everton that offered spectacular views across the Mersey. William Gregson, Mayor in 1762, is one of these, he lived near the corner of Low Hill and West Derby Road and when his old house was demolished in the 19th century to make way for terraced streets, one of them was named **Gregson Street**. Another was **Plumpton Street**, after the Plumptons who owned land in this area during the late 18th and early 19th centuries. William Harper, mayor in 1804 who lived in Rupert Lane (now covered by a recreation ground) is remembered by **Harper Street**, which runs between Erskine Street and Prescot Street. Connecting these two streets at their bottom end is **Moss Street**, which was cut by banker John Moss of Whiston when he bought the land at the beginning of the 19th century. Richard Andrew Mould was a wine merchant who lived in the Kirkdale area. Around 1830 **Mould Street** was laid out in his honour, while parallel to this, **Dalrymple Street** remembers a book keeper and friend of his called William Dalrymple. A merchant named William Lightbody who traded in Dale Street, lived in the area where **Lightbody Street** is now situated.

A timber merchant named Edward Mason moved to Edge Hill and paid for the construction of St. Mary's Church. He built a mansion and laid out **Mason Street** to its south. When the Liverpool to Manchester railway opened, its locomotive terminus was at Edge Hill, with the carriages then being horse drawn to the main station at Crown Street. The first Chairman of the railway company was merchant Charles Lawrence, who had been mayor in 1823 and after whom **Lawrence Road** in Wavertree is named.

Josias Booker was a sugar merchant who had settled in Poplar Grove in Allerton by 1828. He ran plantations in British Guyana and remained a leading figure in Liverpool until his death in 1865. He built some cottages for his farm workers and these became known as Bookers Lane and subsequently its present title of **Booker Avenue**. Thomas Littledale, Mayor in 1826 was buried in Knotty Ash churchyard in 1861. He lived in Highfield House which stood on the site of Broadgreen School. **Littledale**, at the side of the church, is named after him.

LOCAL GOVERNMENT FIGURES
FROM 1835 ONWARDS

I N 1835 THERE WAS A CONSIDERABLE SHAKE UP in Local Government when the Municipal Reform Act standardised council structures across the country. It also stipulated that councillors had to be elected by local ratepayers, as prior to this each authority was able to make its own arrangements. Whereas most mayors from before this Act are remembered in the city centre, those after it tend to be commemorated further afield as Liverpool expanded with time. As well as mayors and councillors, a number of council officials and community members have also been honoured in Liverpool's street names.

One street in the city centre that is named after someone with local government connections is **Eberle Street**. Philip Eberle, who owned two hotels in Dale Street, acted as caterer to the Town Hall for 16 years in the second half of the 19th century after coming to Liverpool from Germany.

One of Liverpool's first Mayors after the 1835 Act was Hugh Hornby, in 1838. He was head of H & J Hornby & Co, which engaged in trade with Russia. Following his stint as Mayor, he went on to become Chairman of the Health Committee. Kent Street North, off Limekiln Lane in Vauxhall, was re-named **Hornby Street** in his honour. This street used to run right through to Vauxhall Road, but has now been considerably shortened by the building of Limekiln Lane Health Centre and Mother Teresa School. On the other side of the school, off Titchfield Street, a small section of the old line of the street remains and is now named **Hornby Walk**.

Following on from Hugh Hornby as Mayor in 1839 was corn merchant Sir Joshua Walmsley. His family owned land in the Vauxhall area and **Walmsley Street** was named after him. He is buried in St Mary's Church in Edge Hill and 140 years after his death a new development there, **Joshua Place**, is being named after him. At this time, Liverpool's docks were expanding northwards and a key figure behind this was James Holme, who suggested that land was purchased from the Earl of

Derby. Despite being a councillor, he devoted far more energy to dock activities and off Derby Road, near to Sandon Dock, **Holme Street** remembers him.

Off Shaw Street, **Langsdale Street** was named after Alderman Edward Langsdale, a timber merchant who lived in Shaw Street. He represented the Everton ward and was Chairman of the Health Committee for many years in the mid 19th century prior to his death in 1857, as well as being a member of the Dock Committee. Near to Liverpool FC's Anfield stadium is **Houlding Street**, named after the man who founded the club, John Houlding. A brewer by trade, Houlding was also a councillor and owned the Sandon Hotel, which is situated on the corner of the street. **Robson Street** in Anfield was named after Edward Robert Robson, who was borough surveyor in the 1860s. John Farnworth was a timber merchant and representative for South Toxteth who was Mayor in 1865, giving his name to **Farnworth Street**.

Richard C. Gardner, who was Mayor in 1862, had lived at Newsham House for some time after Liverpool Corporation purchased it in 1846. When Newsham Park was developed in the 1860s one of its main roads, **Gardners Drive**, was named after him. The much smaller **Gardner Road**, at the bottom end of West Derby Road, also remembers him. His sister Margaret married William Preston, a local councillor who had served as Mayor in 1858. They lived on the other side of Rocky Lane to Newsham Park in Rock House, which gave its name to **Rock House Street**. Just a few streets further up Rocky Lane are **Preston Grove** and **Ellel Grove**. The latter is named after Ellel Grange, an Italianate villa built by Preston in 1859 on land he purchased south of Lancaster. This house is now a listed building and the home of Ellel Ministries, a Christian Missionary Organisation. Nearby there is a **Grange Street**, as well as **Morecambe Street**, which is named after the nearest seaside town to Ellel Grange.

Sheil Road is named after Richard Sheil, a merchant who was the first Irish Alderman on Liverpool Council. **Holt Road** takes its name from George Holt, a councillor for West Derby who was born in Rochdale in 1790 and was a successful property developer. He was responsible for the first India Buildings in 1834 and co-founded the Lamport and Holt shipping line and the Bank of Liverpool. Holt Road was developed on land owned by his father-in-law, wine merchant William Durning, after whom **Durning Road** is named. Durning, Holt and Sheil Roads formed part of Liverpool's first ring road, which was developed in the 1860s to link the southern suburbs of Edge Hill and Toxteth with the northern ones of Anfield and Everton.

In Wavertree part of the old Wavertree Lane was re-named **Picton Road** in honour of councillor, architect and historian Sir James Allanson Picton. He lived in Wavertree and was Chairman of the Libraries and Museums Committee for nearly forty years, being knighted in 1881 for his public services. Two small streets off Picton Road are **Picton Crescent** and **Picton Grove**. After his wife Sarah died in 1879 he dedicated Picton Clock Tower, which was unveiled in 1884, to her.

In the 19th century, a number of local libraries were developed in Liverpool Corporation, five of which were funded by steel magnate and philanthropist Andrew Carnegie (1835-1919). One of those was Lister Drive which closed in 2006 for health and safety reasons, which is adjacent to **Carnegie Road**. Born in Scotland, he emigrated from there to America when he was just 13 and went on to give over $350 million to educational and cultural projects worldwide, including 3,000 libraries.

John Woodruff was a councillor who owned a flourishing pawn broking business, as well as being a senior churchwarden of St Paul's church in Princes Park. Nearby, **Woodruff Street**, off Harlow Street is named after him. Another key pillar of St. Paul's church in the mid 19th century was James Robertson, who traded in timber and represented South Toxteth. **Robertson Street** remembers him, while Charles Henry Beloe, a civil engineer who represented Abercromby Ward from 1892 to 1902, was commemorated when Bright Street was changed to **Beloe Street** in his honour.

In 1879 the Crown Prince of Sweden visited Liverpool and unveiled the Steble Fountain at the top of William Brown Street, which was erected following a donation by Lieutenant-Colonel Steble, Mayor in 1875 after whom **Steble Street**, is named. Nearby, **Bowring Street** and **Bowring Close** are named after another councillor who made a much larger scale donation to the city. William Benjamin Browning presented the Roby Hall Estate for use by the people of Liverpool in 1907. From this Bowring Park was created and is now a golf course, with **Bowring Park Road** leading to it. Bowring was the first elected

Lord Mayor of Liverpool in 1894, having joined the council in 1884 following in his father's footsteps. He was also head of C.T.Bowring & Co. ship owners, a company that is still in existence today under the umbrella of a much larger corporation.

Francis Shand was Mayor in 1856. His father, William Shand had built Springwood House and owned forty acres of land in Allerton. Their merchanting concern traded in Barbados and **Shand Street** in Garston is named in the family's honour.

During the first half of the 20th century, as Liverpool expanded further outward, rural areas such as Walton became swamped with new housing. A number of the main arterial routes built to serve these new estates were named after local civic dignitaries of the time. **Utting Avenue** and **Utting Avenue East** take their names from Sir John Utting, who was Mayor in 1917. He had served on the council from 1899 and was Chairman of the Hospitals Committee, taking a personal interest in the building of Fazakerley Hospital. A doctor, he wrote many papers concerning sanitary science and was also chairman of the Port Sanitary Authority. **Muirhead Avenue** and **Muirhead Avenue East** are named after William Muirhead, Chairman of the Health Committee in the early 20th century. Prior to its development, Muirhead Avenue was a tree lined entrance to Lark Hill Mansion, which stood on its corner with Queens Drive.

As Walton was developed, a famous local figure was remembered in **Richard Kelly Drive**. Kelly was born in Walton in 1839 and served as the local churchwarden, overseer and as a member of the local Conservative Association. He sat on the Walton Urban District Council and when Walton was absorbed into Liverpool he then represented Warbreck on the city council. In addition to all these duties he was also appointed a J.P. in 1893.

In the south of the city, two major routes are also named after former councillors. Alderman Thomas Menlove (1840-1913) was a Chairman of the Health Committee and gives his name to **Menlove Avenue**, which was once no more than a minor track to Woolton. Liverpool's Mayor in 1915, solicitor Arthur Stanley Mather is remembered by **Mather Avenue**. In the mid 19th century councillor and ironmonger Joseph Cooper lived in Oak House on Aigburth Hall Avenue. His memory lives on in **Cooper Avenue North** and **Cooper Avenue**

South, while in the same vicinity **Brodie Avenue** is named after John Alexander Brodie, who was the City Engineer from 1898 to 1925. He developed Queens Drive, but also worked further afield and was responsible for the road system in New Delhi. A keen sports fan, he also patented football goal nets in 1890. An Irish councillor named Gregory Taggart gave his name to **Taggart Avenue** in Childwall after the district was absorbed into Liverpool in 1913. Originally this was called Park Road, after Stand Park, but the name was changed to avoid confusion with Park Road in Liverpool 8.

The naming of streets after councillors has still taken place in much more modern times. In the late 1980s **Paul Orr Court** was built in the Eldonian Village. This was named after Paul Orr, a long-standing councillor for the Vauxhall area. He continued to serve the local community and even after resigning from the Labour Party he still stood as an independent candidate in May 2000, despite being over 80 years old. However, he was beaten into second place in the poll. Paul Orr donated the upturned beer crates that were used as chairs in Liverpool FC's famous 'bootroom', having given trainer Joe Fagan some stout as a thank you for allowing his amateur team to receive treatment at Anfield. He died in 2005.

Rosemary (Rosie) Cooper, after whom **Rosemary Close** off Grove Street is named, was elected to the city council in 1973 aged just 22. She was Lord Mayor 1992-3 and while in office a large-scale re-development programme in that area, Project Rosemary, was put into operation. This included the building of the Liverpool Women's Hospital, of which she became the Chair. Rosie left the council in 2000 and in 2005 was elected to Parliament as MP for West Lancashire.

Although not a councillor, a local community activist and founder member of the West Everton Community Council, Wendy Chase, was honoured by **Chase Way** during the 1990s after the demolition of high rise properties in Netherfield Road. Wendy was a well known local community activist and member of the Islington Tenants Association who played a part in helping re-develop the area after the tenements were knocked down and ensuring the community was not broken up. A well known man from the Vauxhall area, Jim Clarke, was remembered by **James Clarke Way** in the 1980s. Originally from Guyana, Jim came to Liverpool in 1900 and used his swimming ability to save dozens of people over the years from the Leeds & Liverpool canal.

A good all round athlete, he was also a respected community worker. In Anfield, redevelopment of the Pinehurst Estate saw the creation of **Petra Close**, not named after a person, but after the Pinehurst Estate Tenants and Residents Association.

MARITIME INFLUENCES

L IVERPOOL'S DOCK SYSTEM was developed in the 18th century, with canals then being built to transport goods from inland for export. In addition, shipbuilding flourished as merchants required more and more vessels. With the onset of steam in the 19th century, great shipping lines were formed in the city, transporting freight and passengers to all corners of the world. Sadly, the canals have fallen into disuse, the nearest shipyards are now in Birkenhead and air travel has now vastly reduced the numbers of ships seen on the Mersey. However, street names have left us with many reminders of Liverpool's shipbuilding past around the city, as well as of canals and the great liners that sailed from the port around the turn of the 19th century.

Liverpool's first dock engineer was Thomas Steers, who built the first dock in 1715. This involved the draining of the Pool, leading to the formation of **Paradise Street**. Steers, who owned this land, named it after a street in Rotherhithe, London where he once lived. He has recently been commemorated in the Liverpool One development with **Thomas Steers Way**, whilst a section of the dock excavated in 2001 has now been preserved as an attraction. A shipwright, Thomas Hurst, who provided timber for construction of the dock is remembered by **Hurst Street** while a descendant of Steers, Spencer, is commemorated by **Spencer Street** and **Steers Street** in Everton.

Steer's successor was Henry Berry, who lived at the top of Duke Street and is remembered by **Berry Street**. He masterminded the Sankey Canal, which linked Liverpool with St. Helens and gave its name to **Sankey Street**. Perhaps the most famous dock engineer was Jesse Hartley in the mid 19th century. His most best known work is the Albert Dock and one of its roadways, **Hartley Quay**, remembers its builder. **Mathew Street**, famous worldwide as the birthplace of The Beatles, was initially called Pluckington's Alley but in the middle of the 18th century its name changed to Matthew Street after Matthew Pluckington, a mariner who lived there. During the late 19th century one of the 't's has been dropped from the Matthew.

Francis Egerton, 3rd Duke of Bridgewater, developed Dukes Dock in 1773 to export his textiles. The road leading to this, **Gower**

Street, is named after his brother-in-law Granville Leveson-Gower, while **Bridgewater Street** was named after the completion of the Bridgewater Canal that linked Liverpool to Manchester in 1776. This was an extension of an earlier canal, which had been built to carry coal from Bridgewater's mines in Worsley to his factories in Manchester. **Brindley Street** remembers James Brindley, the surveyor of both the Bridgewater Canal and the Trent and Mersey Canal.

The Leeds and Liverpool Canal connected Liverpool with Leeds and the mill towns of Lancashire and Yorkshire. Originally running as far as Old Hall Street, for many years it terminated at Burlington Street before the recent extension to the Pier Head and Albert Dock. It gave its name to **Leeds Street**, which was developed in the late 19th century on the site of a former road called Maidens Green. Nearby, there had been another Leeds Street named after the canal, which then became **Old Leeds Street**. Nearly 100 years later in the 1980s new developments in the Vauxhall area were **Canalside Grove** and **Lockfields View**. One of the commodities carried along the canal was cotton, giving rise to **Cotton Street** which had originally been called William Street and was renamed in the middle of the 19th century. Redevelopment of the Princes Dock area in the mid 2000s has seen the creation of **William Jessop Way**. This is named after William Jessop (1745-1814), a canal engineer whose contributions to local development are the Ellesmere Canal, linking Ellesmere Port with Chester, and the Chester Canal linking Nantwich with the River Dee.

Grayson Street is named after a shipwright called Edward Grayson, whose works, H & C Grayson were on the site of the Albert Dock. Grayson, who was Mayor in 1770, was killed in a duel in 1804, the last but one to be fought in Liverpool. His killer was William Sparling, whose family are remembered in nearby **Sparling Street**, which was in existence by 1785 and named after a Mr Sparling's shipyard. Also in this area is **Carpenters Row**, which commemorates the carpenters who worked in the local shipyards. One of the many uses for ships built in 18th Century Liverpool was the whaling industry. Baffin Street, which is no longer in existence, ran alongside Queens Dock, where ships would have come back to with their catch. This was named after Baffin Bay, off the Greenland coast. However, there is still a **Greenland Street**, running off St. James Street in the direction of Queens Dock. These streets were so named as the whaling trade started to look further away for its catch after supplies near Norway became exhausted.

In the 2nd quarter of the 19th century William Laird developed Birkenhead almost single handed. After first living in Liverpool when he came down to England from Scotland, he realised the potential of the Wirral side of the Mersey and moved there in 1824, opening his first shipyard at Wallasey Pool in 1828. Liverpool did not forget him however and **Laird's Place**, off Burlington Street in Vauxhall is named after him.

On the Springwood Estate in Allerton there is a **Brocklebank Lane**. This takes its name from Thomas Brocklebank who lived in Springwood House from 1844 to 1906. He had acquired his wealth through his grandfather, who had built shipyards in Whitehaven in the 18th century. Another member of the family was Ralph Brocklebank, who was Chairman of the Mersey Docks and Harbour Board from 1863 to 1869 and was succeeded on his retirement by Thomas Langton, a partner in T & W Earle American merchants. He was also Chairman of the Pacific Steamship Company and **Langton Street** in Wavertree is named after him.

As the 19th century wore on, shipping lines rather than shipbuilders became more prominent in Liverpool, as the passenger trade grew. One example of a yard to close was Thomas Royden & Sons, which had been started in 1818 by Thomas Royden after he came to Liverpool as a 16 years old shipyards apprentice in 1808. His company was situated on the site of the Queens Dock Customs and Excise Building and developed into a nationwide leader in the construction of large iron sailing ships. In the late 19th century his son, Thomas Bland Royden closed it down and then founded the Indra Line of steamships, which traded between London and New Zealand, the Far East and USA. The Royden family are remembered by **Royden Way**, which leads into the Brunswick Business Park, built on the site of Toxteth and Harrington Docks, giving rise to **Harrington Road**. Other shipping lines to be commemorated here are **Harrison Way** and **Ellerman Road**, named after the Harrison and Ellerman Lines respectively. The former operated to the West Indies from Toxteth Dock and the Americas connections are also shown here by **Atlantic Way** and **Columbus Quay**, named after the Atlantic Ocean and Christopher Columbus who discovered the West Indies in 1492.

In 1840, the first Cunard service out of Liverpool left bound for Halifax and Boston and the company later had their headquarters in the Cunard Building on the waterfront. Cunard's influence in Liverpool can be seen in Walton, where a small group of streets are named after their ships. **Ivernia Road** and **Saxonia Road** are named after sister ships which sailed between Liverpool and Boston, while **Sylvania Road** takes its name from a ship that carried cargo on the same route. **Lusitania Road** and **Mauretania Road** are named after two 'superliners' that took passengers from Liverpool to New York. The *Mauretania* held the westbound and eastbound speed crossing records for twenty years until 1929 while the *Lusitania*, which was the largest vessel in the world when launched in 1906, was torpedoed off the coast of Ireland in 1915. This act by a German U-boat cost 1,200 lives and led to Cunard suspending Atlantic passenger services during the First World War.

In Garston, more Cunard ships that sailed between Liverpool and America have been remembered. **Campania Street** and **Lucania Street** are named after sister ships that were the largest in the world when built in 1893. The *Lucania* was destroyed by fire in Huskisson Dock in 1909 while the *Campania* sank after a collision with a battleship in 1918 following its sale to the navy for use as a troop-ship. Two other sister ships are remembered by **Etruria Street** and **Umbria Street**. They were the last Cunard ships to have sails and remained in service until being scrapped in 1910. **Carpathia Street** is named after a ship most famous for rescuing survivors from the *Titanic*, while **Caronia Street** takes its name from one of the first ships in the world to be fitted with watertight doors. All the ships mentioned so far carried passengers from Liverpool to New York, but one liner that sailed from Liverpool to Boston gives its name to **Ultonia Street**. This ship was a cargo steamer on the route but after moving to the Trieste-New York route in 1904, it eventually sank after being hit by a German torpedo in 1917, all bar one of the people on board being saved.

Cunard's great rival was the White Star Line, whose ships are not so well represented in the city. **Oceanic Road** in Old Swan is named after their first passenger ship, which was launched in 1871 and sailed on the Liverpool to New York route. Another shipping line based in Liverpool was the City of Dublin Steam Packet Company, which ran passenger and mail services between Liverpool and Ireland. Their berth was near to **Dublin Street**, while in Old Swan four of the company's ships are remembered by **Belfast Road**, **Leinster Road**, **Munster Road** and **Ulster Road**.

When an old school playing field off Chelwood Avenue was developed in the 1990s, a number of the streets were named after other ports. They are **Dover Grove**, **Harwich Grove**, **Peacehaven Close** and **Castletown Close**, the latter in the Isle of Man having stopped commercial operations in the 1970s.

LIVERPOOL'S BIG HOUSES

As Liverpool became more crowded during the late 18th Century, many merchants began to move away from the town to countryside areas such as Everton or Wavertree. These houses were usually built near to main roads so they could still get to Liverpool quite easily when necessary. With the onset of railways in the 19th century, wealthy traders were able to move even further away from the inner city area and commute to their business premises. Many of these large houses are still in existence today, or alternatively leave their legacy behind in the naming of streets.

West India merchant George Campbell built an ecclesiastic looking mansion in Everton and named it St Domingo House after a French ship he had captured off the coast of San Domingo. The house was demolished after Campbell's death in 1773, but John Sparling built another in its place and lived there until his death in 1800. The property was then leased out by his son and eventually became a school. Situated on its corner with Beacon Lane, it gave its name to St. Domingo Lane, which was then an unnamed continuation north of Heyworth Street and is now known as **St Domingo Road**. The estates grounds stretched as far as Walton Breck Road and **St Domingo Vale** and **St Domingo Grove** also take their names from the house. James Atherton purchased part of the estate around Heyworth Street and developed Grecian Terrace and York Terrace. In the 20th century he was remembered when **Atherton Close** was built.

Although there is a water tower in Everton, **Waterhouse Street** is not connected to it. Instead it is named after Nicholas Waterhouse, a Quaker who lived in a mansion here in the early 19th century, with the lane leading to it taking his name. **Gleave Square** and the more recently developed **Gleave Crescent** recall a mansion that stood on Everton Road that had been built in the 19th century by a Dr Gleave. A wine merchant, Samuel Woodhouse owned a house called Bronte near to Everton Valley, which gave its name to **Bronte Street** off London Road.

Stonehill Avenue and **Springbank Road** in Anfield are named after Stone Hill House and Spring Bank House respectively, which both stood at their corners with Oakfield Road (then named Upper Belmont Road) until they made way for the new housing in the late 19th century. Also in Anfield, Anfield House stood on the site of what is now the Arkles pub. In 1871 banker George Arkle lived here, giving rise to **Arkles Road** and **Arkles Lane**. These are near to **Walton Breck Road**, **Breck Road** and **Breckfield Road North and South**. The term 'breck' refers to an area of uncultivated land, reflecting the districts rural origins. Breckfield House and Breckfield Lodge stood near the corner of Breck Road and Breckfield Road North and was demolished in the 1870s to make way for **Thirlmere Road**, named after Lake Thirlmere in Cumbria. Other streets off this were named after lakes and the area became known as the 'Lake District'. They are **Coniston Street, Grasmere Street, Rydal Street, Ullswater Street** and **Windermere Street**.

In Tuebrook, the Larkhill mansion was built for merchant and colliery owner Jonathan Blundell. It was purchased by banker Richard Heywood in 1776 and remained in his family's hands for over one hundred years, before becoming a branch library for Liverpool City Council. It was demolished in 1962 but has given its name to **Larkhill Lane**. One of the lanes within the estate was **Lisburn Lane**, which is still in existence today, being named as it led to Lisburn Farm. A house called Barnfield used to exist on the site of the Jolly Miller pub on Queens Drive. This is remembered today by **Barnfield Drive**, which came into existence shortly after the 2nd World War. The Jolly Miller's name originates from the ancient mill that stood at the top of **Millbank**. This mill gave its name to a house and subsequently the road of the same name.

In 1855 Russian consul Philip Blessig built Blackmoor Hall on the site of Blackmoor Moss in West Derby. This was demolished in the 1920s, giving rise to **Blackmoor Drive**. A Georgian house in West Derby came into the hands of Lawrence Heyworth, a merchant, in the early 19th century. He built a tree house in a yew tree in its garden and the house where he lived then became known as Yew Tree House. This then gave the name to the road it stood on, **Yew Tree Lane**. Another merchants house in West Derby was Bellefield, once owned by East India merchant Sir Edward Bates. **Bellefield Drive** was named after this, but it was closed off from Sandfield Park as Bates refused to pay for the upkeep of roads there in return for access to it. It remains like this today.

Scarisbrick House stood in Norris Green and was owned by the Scarisbrick family of Scarisbrick Hall, near Ormskirk. **Scarisbrick Crescent**, **Scarisbrick Drive**, **Scarisbrick Road** and **Scarisbrick Place** all take their names from this house. The road on which it was situated, **Strawberry Road**, took its name from Strawberry Farm in the early 19th Century, although it was then known as Strawberry Lane. In Fazakerley, **Sparrow Hall Road** does not take its named from a grand property. Sparrow Hall was a black and white cottage that stood on the corner of Long Lane and Lower Lane, but nicknamed such due to the birds that used to nest in its thatched roof.

Spellow Lane in Walton takes its name from Spellow House, which was owned by the Fazakerley family of Fazakerley Hall in Lower Lane. Spellow House was built in the 13th century, not demolished until 1860 and its name has origins from Viking times 1,000+ years ago. The word spellow is a Scandinavian term meaning meeting hill and the house was built where once the Vikings would have made announcements. **Fazakerley Road** was the original driveway to Fazakerley House, a three storey stone farmhouse built in 1749. **Evered Avenue** remembers Miss Evered, who owned the house at the start of the 20th century and was a relative of the Fazakerley family. The house, along with its grounds, was subsequently sold to Liverpool Corporation and demolished. The Rice family, who were related by marriage to the Fazakerleys, had a house called Rice House, which stood close to the Breeze Hill flyover. **Rice Lane** remembers the family and house.

The original name for **Hall Lane** in Edge Hill was Mount Vernon, named due to its slope and its proximity to Vernon's Hall, a 18th century or earlier structure. The name was changed in the mid 19th century but the name of the long gone hall has survived in a number of smaller streets in the area bearing the name, the most significant of which is **Mount Vernon**.

A doctor named Samuel Solomon, who practised in Marybone developed a herbal medicine named the 'balm of gilead' in the early 19th century, which he produced from a secret recipe. Gilead is actually two Hebrew words, meaning 'eternal joy'. He built a mansion named Gilead House, off Kensington, from the proceeds of this. When this was demolished **Balm Street**, **Gilead Street** and **Solomon Street** were named in his honour. Elms House, that stood near the junction of Edge Lane and St Oswald Street in Old Swan was only demolished around the turn of the millennium after falling into a derelict state. **Elms House Road** had taken its name from this and a small cul de sac called **Elmway** was built on the site of the house.

In Broadgreen, merchant Joseph Leigh built Oak Hill House in 1773, standing between what is now Rossall Road and Saville Road. It was named after some oak trees were brought here from the ladies walk, a tree line walk exclusive to ladies, in Old Hall Street in 1778. The last tenant of the house was timber merchant Edward Chaloner. The house was demolished in the early 20th century and its name lives on in **Oakhill Park**, **Oakhill Road** and **West Oakhill Park**. The Newsham Molineux family, who are commemorated by **Molineux Avenue**, owned the Staplands mansion, after which **Staplands Road** is named. However, their main residence was at Newsham Park and **Molyneux Road**, off Sheil road remembers them there. This family is no relation to the Molyneux family who were the Earls of Sefton and lived at Croxteth Hall.

Part of the Newsham Park estate was sold for building development in the 1840s. This led to the building of **Tynwald Hill**, named after the Isle of Man parliament and coming from a word that means 'assembly field'. More recent developments here are **Tynwald Close** and **Tynwald Place**, while the Isle of Man theme continues with **Douglas Close**, named after the island's capital.

The district of Dovecot takes its name from Dovecote House, built in 1829 by John Tarbock on the junction of Pilch Lane and **Dovecot Avenue**, which also has a **Dovecot Place** off it. It was later occupied by a cotton merchant named Adam Dugdale and had been named after an earlier house of the same name which was demolished in the 18th century. The name dovecote comes from a building, which would have been used by the lord of the manor for housing doves, which were a source of winter food. Richard Gildart built Finch House in 1776 after buying land from the Earl of Sefton. Mockbeggar Lane, on which it stood, then became **Finch Lane**. The house was eventually demolished in 1912 after coming into the hands of the Earls of Derby and **Finch Dene**, **Finch Way** and **Finch Close** also take their names from it.

James Clements, who was Mayor in 1775 built Ashfield House off the 'road to Wavertree' (later Picton Road). **Ashfield** takes its name from this, as well as **Ash Grove**, **Ash Close** and **Ash Vale**.

Wavertree playground was created in 1895 following the anonymous donation of a derelict house and its grounds called 'The Grange' to the City of Liverpool. This is why the playing fields are often referred to as 'The Mystery'. The house, in which Prince Alfred, son of Queen Victoria, stayed in 1866 was demolished in 1895 but **Grange Terrace** means its name still lives on. **Lance Lane** took its name from Lance Cottage, which was named by insurance broker Thomas Lance (1769-1829). **Heathfield Road** was named after Heathfield, a house owned in the early 20th century by solicitor William Watson Rutherford (see also 'Liverpool's MPs and Prime Ministers').

A public inquiry in 1998 was held into the future of Sandown Hall in Olive Lane, Wavertree, as its new owners wanted to demolish it for new housing. Two years later, Deputy Prime Minister John Prescott reluctantly gave the go ahead for this as the hall had fallen into disrepair and it was demolished in November 2000. Built in the early 1800s, it came into the hands of Crawford Biscuits in the 1920s for use as its sports and social club. The hall gave its name to Sandown Park, a private 19th century residential estate containing a number of mansions. **Sandown Road** takes its name from the estate while **Crawford Drive** is in relation to its one time owner. **Sandown Lane**, which leads to the Sandown Park estate, was first proposed in 1803 but it was some years before it got developed. Its varying stages of development mean that many different architectural styles are featured in the road. One of the developments, Alma Terrace, was built by William Pearson, who is remembered on the other side of Picton Road by **Pearson Street**.

A mansion called Westdale House used to stand at the junction of Rathbone Road and Sunningdale Road. Its last owner was cotton broker John Stock and after 1910, new roads were laid out including **Westdale Road**. The dale theme continues as **Eastdale Road**, **Northdale Road** and **Southdale Road** all took their names from this one house, as do **Mindale Road**, **Standale Road** and **Sunningdale Road**. Valencia House, which made way for **Valencia Road** in the 1930s, was once the home of a fruit broker named William M. George, who may have named it after the Spanish city of Valencia that is an important centre for agricultural trading.

In 1790 Olive Mount House was built. Now used as health authority offices, it is not certain what was named first, Olive Mount hill or house. The house has given its name to **Olive Mount Road** and **Olive Mount Walk**, while its surrounding buildings, which formed a children's hospital, were demolished in the 1990s to make way for **Crossley Drive**, **Hollins Close** and **Swan Crescent**. These three new streets were named at the suggestion of the local Wavertree Society after Luke Crossley, who lived there in 1841, Francis Hollins, a cotton broker who lived there in 1871 and James Swan, a tea dealer who built the house.

Eton Lodge in Childwall has been a home for Catholic bishops since 1851, but its intended purpose when it was built 75 years earlier was as a school, the 'Eton of the North'. **Cromptons Lane** is named after Dr. Peter Crompton, one of its former owners. Dudlow Hall gave is name to **Dudlow Lane**, **Dudlow Drive** and **Dudlow Gardens**, while **Dudlow Nook Road** now marks the edge of what was the Dudlow Estate. At the top of Taggart Avenue was Stand House, which is now the site of shops. The land surrounding the house was known as Stand Park and is now a Liverpool Hope campus, but its name lives on in **Stand Park Road**, the park being added given that was what Taggart Avenue was once known as. Another large house, Hill Top stood at the top of Childwall Priory Road. This was once the home of Colonel Henry Concanon, Assistant General Manager of the White Star Line. When the house was demolished before the 2nd World War, **Hilltop Road** was named in its memory.

The district of Belle Vale takes its name from Belle Vale Hall, which stood at the corner of Wambo Lane and **Belle Vale Road**. Lee Hall, which stood on the site of Lee Park golf course, was built for ship builder John Okill in 1773 and demolished in 1956. One of its residents during the 19th century was John Hayes Wilson, a Chairman of the Liverpool Water Committee who was involved in the construction of Liverpool' s main water supply at Lake Vrynwy The hall gives its name to the surrounding district as well as **Lee Hall Road**.

The Grange mansion on Rose Brow, Gateacre was re-built in 1865 on the site of an earlier house by Sir Andrew Barclay Walker. He was Mayor of Liverpool in 1873, 1876 and 1877, as well as being the owner of Walkers Warrington brewery. He also gave money for the building of the Walker Art Gallery in William Brown Street in the city centre. The Grange has now been converted into apartments, having previously been used as a seaman's home, hence **Seafarers Way**. Gateacre Hall was situated at the bottom of **The Nook**, which was the original name for the hall until its demolition in 2003 to make way for new housing. The former name for the Grange Manor (now a function suite) was Gorsey Cop, which is still remembered by **Gorsey Cop Road** and **Gorsey Cop Way**. Other houses, which are now long demolished, that have given their names to streets in Gateacre are Elmsfield, (**Elmsfield Close**) and Orient House, (**Orient Drive**).

In Woolton, a local solicitor by the name of Ambrose Lee laid out **Beaconsfield Road** in the 1860s to lead to his mansion, Beaconsfield. Off Menlove Avenue, **The Vineries** is named after an estate that was once the residence of a Thomas Charles Clarke and was unfit for occupation by the early 20th century. Many of the houses in the Woolton and Gateacre area were built using stone from Woolton Quarry, which was opened by James Rose, a self made man who was born in 1783 and married well. The quarry is still remembered by **Quarry Street**, **The Old Quarry** and **Rockmount Close**, while Rose himself built **Rose Street**. **Ridgetor Road** also takes its name from the quarry, being a combination of two words meaning long peak and rocky hill Another quarry owner and builder in this area in the middle of the 19th century was John Greenough, after whom **Greenough Street** was named. Quarrying continued in Woolton until the late 1970s when the Anglican Cathedral was finally completed. After this the last of the quarry was filled in and **Clay Cross Road** built.

In 1847 merchant Joseph Hornby purchased some land east of Menlove Avenue. A house was then designed by Lonsdale Elmes and named Druids Cross House, presumably due to the proximity of the Calder Stones, which may be 3-4,000 years old. **Druids Cross Road** was formally adopted in 1868 and the house has also given its name to **Druids Cross Gardens**, **Druids Park** and **Druidsville Road,** while **Hornby Lane** commemorated Joseph Hornby himself.

The Harthill Estate, which is now Liverpool's botanic gardens, is in Calderstones Park. In the grounds of this stood Harthill House, which was built in 1825 and has given its name to **Harthill Avenue** and **Harthill Road**. This was bought in 1848 by iron and copper merchant John Bibby, son-in-law of dock engineer Jesse Hartley. After his death in 1899 it became a police headquarters before its demolition in 1937 after dry rot was found.

The **Allerton Beeches** mansion, which gives its name to a road of the same name, was demolished in 1939, having been built for sugar refiner Sir Henry Tate (1819-99). This mansion was built on the site of another large house called Greenhill, after which **Greenhill Road** is named. Further down Allerton Road, opposite Yew Tree Road, stood **Verdala Towers**, another house that is copied by a road name. Its first tenant, Charles McIver Junior in 1870, gave the house its unusual name, naming it after a tower in Malta that literally means 'tower of the greenfields.' **Yew Tree Road** was laid out as a private road by Ambrose Lace in 1864 and named after Yew Tree Farm. Off this road is **Dowsefield Lane**, which led to Dowsefield, a house built by a civil engineer, Hermann J. Sillemm and named after Dowse House farm.

The origins of **Carnatic Road** in Mossley Hill go back to 1778 when a French ship, the *Carnatic,* was captured by a privateering vessel called the *Mentor,* captained by John Dawson. The prize included raw silk, coffee and tea and from the proceeds of this Peter Baker, owner of the *Mentor,* was able to build Carnatic Hall. This hall burnt down in 1889 and a new one built on its site, which was pulled down in 1964 to make way for the University of Liverpool student residences that bear the same name. Within the grounds of Carnatic Hall stood Elmswood Hall, which now gives its name to **Elmswood Road**. This road was in existence in the 18th century as an unnamed lane that connected to Rose Lane.

Also in Mossley Hill, **Briarwood Road** takes its name from a house of the same name that stood on Carnatic Road. At the turn of the 20th century Joseph Ainsworth Woods, a dental surgeon, lived there. Nearby, **Kelton Grove** is named after a house still in existence, which is now a Nugent Care training centre. **North Sudley Road** was re-named along with **South Sudley Road** after the creation of a sports ground on Barkhill Road split the original Sudley Road in two. This was named after Sudley Hall, which is now an art gallery. The hall was purchased by shipping magnate George Holt (see Holt Road) in 1883 and was left to the city of Liverpool by his daughter Emma Holt in 1944 after she died leaving no siblings. **Pitville Road** and **Pitville Avenue** take their names from a house called Pitville, which stood on the site of the University Sports Ground that the roads now surround.

Two buildings now owned by Liverpool John Moores University gave their names to **Barkhill Road** and **Holmefield Road**. Irene M.

Marsh purchased the mansion of Barkhill in the early 20th century for her training college for women physical education teachers. It later became known as the I.M. Marsh College and expanded in 1947 when Holmefield House, a grade II listed building once occupied by shipping magnate and MP Sir Thomas Bland Royden, was purchased. The college became part of the then Liverpool Polytechnic in 1983 and although this became Liverpool John Moores University in 1992, the I.M. Marsh College has retained a separate identity within it. Elm Hall stood near the corner of Allerton Road and Penny Lane, with its estate stretching down to Queens Drive Mossley Hill. It is remembered now by **Elm Hall Drive.**

The Elms in Toxteth was named after a house of the same name. The house was built around 1840 and had six elm trees in its grounds. Another mansion in this area was Fairview, which has given its name to **Fairview Place**.

Aigburth Hall was a medieval building that came into the hands of the Tarleton family through marriage. This was demolished around 1840 and a new hall was built which has also since been demolished. The hall, which was once the home of city engineer J.A Brodie gives its name To **Aigburth Hall Avenue** and **Aigburth Hall Road**. Off Aigburth Hall Avenue is **Oakland Road**, its name taken from the Oaklands mansion, home of merchant Richard Harrison from 1810 to 1840. It was also a home of Sir Alfred Lewis Jones, founder of the Liverpool School of Tropical Medicine. The hunting lodge of the mansion still stands on the bend of Holmefield Road, opposite the Grange hotel. Also in Aigburth there is a **Roxburgh Avenue**, named after cotton merchant John Roxburgh who lived in a one of the houses in Aigburth Drive at the beginning of the 20th century, which he named Rowallan.

In 1844 shipbuilder Thomas Brocklebank bought Springwood House from William Shand and lived there until he died in 1906, aged 92. The 121-acre estate was bought by Liverpool Corporation in 1921 for development, but the house itself remains and is now a nursing home. **Springwood Avenue** takes its name from the house. At the turn of the twentieth century, a house called Melbreck stood at the junction of **Melbreck Road** and Greenhill Road. **Cleveley Road** and **Cleveley Park** takes their names from Cleveley, built by cotton merchant Joseph Leather but demolished in 1965.

LIVERPOOL'S MPS
AND PRIME MINISTERS

EOPLE EITHER FROM OR ASSOCIATED WITH LIVERPOOL have made great contributions to national politics. Whether they were born in Liverpool, represented the city or jut owned land locally, they have all had their mark left permanently in local street names.

The earliest Liverpool street to be named after an MP was **Sir Thomas Street**, laid out as Sir Thomas Buildings in the late 17th century on land belonging to Sir Thomas Johnson. Johnson had been Mayor in 1695 and went on to be MP for the town from 1701 to 1723. While at Parliament, he brought in the Bill for the construction of Liverpool's first dock. Although not heavily involved in the slave trade, he was a joint financier of the city's second slave ship the *Blessing* in 1700. The Municipal Buildings are on the site of his house and his memory is preserved in a tablet there. John Hardman was MP for Liverpool when he died in 1755. He had bought Allerton Hall (now a pub/restaurant named the Pub in the Park) and owned land through which **Hardman Street** was later laid. This street was named after his widow Jane, who died in 1795 at the age of 92. She had given a large part of her life to charity after all four of her children died before reaching adulthood.

Gascoyne Street in Vauxhall is named after Isaac Gascoyne, who represented Liverpool in Parliament from 1796 to 1831. Despite campaigns throughout the country for abolition, he continued to defend the slave trade, as he felt it was essential to Liverpool's economy. His brother, Bamber Gascoyne Junior had been MP from 1780 to 1796 and was preceded by Richard Pennant, who served in the Commons from 1767 to 1780. Pennant was also against abolition of the slave trade and was created Lord Penrhyn in 1783, giving his name to **Penrhyn Street** in Everton.

The only central Liverpool MP to become Prime Minister was George Canning, who in 1827 held the post for 4 months until his death. He had earlier been Foreign Secretary and Leader of the House of Commons. In the 1830s **Canning Street** was developed in his honour, while down near the waterfront **Canning Place** remembers him.

One of the most famous MPs to be remembered in Liverpool is William Huskisson, after whom **Huskisson Street** was named in the 1830s. He was a local MP from 1822 to 1830 and President of the Board of Trade, a role that enabled him to represent the interests of Liverpool's merchants by reducing duties on cotton and sugar. Unfortunately he has gone down in history more for being the first person to be killed in a railway passenger accident. During the opening of the Liverpool & Manchester Railway in 1830, the train stopped for a break at Parkside, near Newton-le-Willows. He crossed the line to speak to the Prime Minister, the Duke of Wellington but was struck by the locomotive. His injuries were so severe he died later that day. He is buried in a circular tomb, which still stands in St James' Cemetery to the rear of the Anglican Cathedral.

Cresswell Street, off Everton Road, is named after Cresswell Cresswell, a lawyer born in Newcastle who was one of Liverpool's two MPs from 1837 to 1842. Sir Howard Douglas represented the town for the next five years having earlier enjoyed a distinguished naval career that included spending a winter on the coast of Labrador in Canada after being shipwrecked. **Sir Howard Street**, **Sir Howard Way** and **Back Sir Howard Street** in Liverpool 8 remember him.

Dudley Ryder, Viscount Sandon, had been elected MP for Liverpool at the same time as Cresswell Cresswell. Linking Faulkner Street and Upper Parliament Street is **Sandon Street**, while one of the docks developed on the North Shore was also named Sandon Dock to commemorate him. Near to this is **Sandon Way**, which is off Derby Road on the Sandon Industrial Estate. In 1847 Viscount Sandon succeeded the earldom of Harrowby and had to give up his seat in the Commons, but he remained in politics and was later made Chancellor of the Duchy of Lancaster. His son, Dudley, went on to become an MP in Liverpool, from 1868 until he succeeded the earldom on the death of his father in 1882. **Harrowby Street** and **Harrowby Close** in Toxteth are named after him, the latter having originally been part of the street before it was reduced in size.

Despite being born in Ireland and representing South Lancashire in Parliament, William Brown did make his mark in Liverpool. He had come to Liverpool to establish a branch of his father's linen merchants firm and paid for the building of the William Brown Library, laying the foundation stone in 1857. When the building opened in 1860, the street in which it was situated, Shaws Brow, was re-named **William Brown**

Street. The street's previous name had come from Samuel Shaw, who had established an 18th century pottery in the street. The family of Thomas Brassey (1836-1918) who served as MP for Hastings from 1868 to 1884 and unsuccessfully fought for the Abercomby seat a year later is remembered by **Brassey Street** in Toxteth. His father, also Thomas was a railway contractor who was born in Chester and lived in Birkenhead. He built lines all over the world, including Africa and India and left £3.2 million in his will when he died in 1870.

Born in Liverpool, William Ewart Gladstone had four terms as Prime Minister between 1868 and 1894, more than any other. **Gladstone Street**, off Vauxhall Road is named after him, as is a street of the same name in Edge Hill. There is also a **Gladstone Road** in Walton and Garston. Near to Gladstone Road in Garston, a Merseyside man who went on to become Prime Minister of New Zealand is commemorated by **Seddon Road**. Richard Seddon was born in Eccleston in 1845 and worked in a foundry before emigrating to Australia when he was 18 and moving on to New Zealand when he was 21. Despite being mocked on occasions when he went into politics for having had a poor education and dropping his 'h's, he wasn't deterred and became Prime Minister in 1893, holding office until he died suddenly in 1906.

Edward Whitley served as leader of the Conservatives on Liverpool council before his election in 1880 as MP for Everton. **Whitley Street** in Vauxhall remembers him. George Goschen, who had earlier served as Chancellor of the Exchequer, was elected MP for Liverpool Exchange in 1887. He is remembered in Anfield and Old Swan, which both have a **Goschen Street**. William Watson Rutherford was a solicitor who lived in Wavertree and was Lord Mayor of Liverpool in 1902. The following year he was elected MP for West Derby and **Rutherford Road**, off Queens Drive in Mossley Hill, is named after him.

The 3rd Marquis of Salisbury, Robert Gascoyne Cecil, owner of Childwall Hall was Prime Minister from 1886 to 1892 and 1895 to 1902. He is not commemorated in the immediate city centre area (Salisbury Street near Islington is named after his forefathers), but in Wavertree a number of streets are named after him, the most obvious ones being **Salisbury Road** and **Cecil Street**. George Cadogan, 5th Earl Cadogan served under Salisbury during both his periods as Prime Minister, first as Lord Privy Seal and secondly as Lord Lieutenant of Ireland. He is remembered by **Cadogan Street** that adjoins Cecil Street.

Cranbourne Road takes its name from the title of Viscount Cranborne that was given to the marquis of Salisbury's eldest son. Cecil had assumed this in 1865 on the death of his elder brother James. **Alderson Road** is named in honour of his wife, Georgina Alderson, while **Childwall Avenue** commemorates Childwall Hall, which had been built in the 18th century by Bamber Gascoyne. The hall was sold to Liverpool Corporation in 1947 but demolished when extensive dry rot was found. Salisbury's son Edgar was given the title Viscount Cecil of Chelwood in 1923 after a 17 year Parliamentary career, during which he served as assistant secretary of state for foreign affairs. He went on to represent British interests in the League of Nations and is remembered in Childwall by **Chelwood Avenue**.

NATIONAL & INTERNATIONAL POLITICIANS

A NUMBER OF LIVERPOOL'S STREETS are named after Prime Ministers and prominent politicians. The pattern follows that of local government figures or MPs, with streets in the city centre being named after earlier figures than those in the suburbs.

The first Prime Minister to be commemorated by a street name in Liverpool city centre was William Pitt The Elder, 1st Earl of Chatham who was in office from 1766 to 1768. **Pitt Street** had been laid out in his honour in 1765, before he became Prime Minister, in recognition of a distinguished military political career that had begun in 1735. A later continuation of Pitt Street was **Upper Pitt Street**. His son, William Pitt the Younger, was Prime Minister from 1783 to 1801 and 1804 to 1806. He died while in office and Great Pitt Street was named in his honour, although this was soon changed to Pomona Street. Around the same time, **Chatham Street** was developed and was perhaps named after his father's title, given the fact that no title had yet been bestowed upon him.

Outside the city centre, an earlier Prime Minister than Pitt the Elder to be remembered was John Stuart, Earl of Bute, who gave his name to **Bute Street** in Everton. He was in office for only eleven months from 1762 to 1763 before being forced to resign due to gossip about his private life, as he had become close to the widow of the Prince of Wales. He was also unpopular in the west and south-west of England due to a tax on cider production. Augustus Henry Fitzroy, the 3rd Duke of Grafton, was another Prime Minister who was forced to resign due to attacks on his private life after three years in office from 1767 to 1770, having got married within two months of a divorce. He gave his name to **Fitzroy Way** in Everton, as well as **Grafton Street** in Toxteth.

Lord North, 2nd Earl of Guilford was Prime Minster from 1770 to 1782, resigning after Britain's defeat in the American War of Independence. **North Street**, off Dale Street is named after him, as is **Back Guilford Street** in Everton, one of a number in the vicinity named after Prime

Ministers of the pre Victorian era. Charles Wentworth succeeded Guilford, but died in office after only a few months allowing William Petty, Marquis of Landsdowne, to take over. Landsdowne restored peace with America and is remembered by **Landsdowne Place**. Robert Banks Jenkinson, 2nd Earl of Liverpool, was Prime Minister from 1812 to 1827, winning four general elections before finally resigning after suffering a stroke. **Jenkinson Street** was named after him. In addition to a number of streets in Everton that are named after Prime Ministers, there is a **Downing Street** and **Premier Street**. The original Downing Street in London takes its name from Sir George Downing who was Secretary of the Treasury in 1667.

Staying in Everton, there are a number of streets that have been named after politicians and members of the public who were active in the campaign for Parliamentary reform in the 18th century, when very few people were allowed to vote. Charles Fox, who was Lord of the Treasury under Lord North, is remembered by **Fox Street**. He was against the slave trade and a promoter of Catholic Emancipation, as at the time Catholics were denied a number of civil rights, including being able to vote. In 1794 he denounced the trial of lawyer John Horne Tooke, who was charged with High Treason after trying to organise a convention for supporters of reform. Tooke, who was found not guilty after the jury were out for just eight minutes, is commemorated in **Horne Street** and there was once a Tooke Street in existence. **Richmond Row** is named after another reformist, Charles Lennox, Duke of Richmond, who tried to introduce a reform bill to Parliament in 1780 but found no support. He testified at the trial of Tooke and was forced to admit his previous radical views for reform and as a result had to resign from his position in the government. One man who fared worse was Scottish reformist William Skirving, after whom **Skirving Street** is named. He was transported to Australia in 1794 for distributing leaflets in Edinburgh urging reform and died of yellow fever soon after arriving there.

Another reformer to be commemorated by a street is philanthropist John Howard (1726-90), who spent most of his adult life touring prisons in Britain and Europe and advising on improvements that would assist with sanitation and the prisoners' physical and mental wellbeing. Today his legacy lives on with The Howard League for Penal Reform and a street running north out of Liverpool city centre, **Great Howard Street**.

William Wyndham Baron Grenville, who introduced the bill to Parliament for the abolition of slavery, served as Prime Minister from 1806 to 1807. **Grenville Street South** in the city centre remembers him, but for a short time in the mid 19th century this was named Leveson Street. This is due to boundary changes in 1835 that saw Everton absorbed into Liverpool. As a Grenville Street existed in Everton, the street name in Liverpool was changed to Leveson Street to avoid confusion. However, after the brutal murder of four people in the street in 1849, the name was changed back and the suffix south added due to the notoriety the street was attracting.

Grenville was succeeded as Prime Minister by William Henry Cavendish Bentinck, 3rd Duke of Portland, who has four streets in the Vauxhall area named after him. They are **Bentinck Street**, **Portland Street**, **Titchfield Street** and **Woodstock Street**. The latter two streets come from two of his other titles, Marquis of Titchfield and Viscount Woodstock. He was Prime Minister from 1807 to 1809 after serving as Home Secretary from 1794 to 1801.

Bentinck's Lord Chancellor was John Scott, 1st Earl of Eldon, who is also remembered in Vauxhall by **Eldon Street**, **Eldon Grove** and **Eldon Place**. He held the position between 1801 and 1827, except for a brief interlude in 1806-7 when Thomas Erskine, 1st Baron Erskine was in the post. Erskine, after whom **Erskine Street** in Everton is named, famously saved a madman who tried to shoot King George III from the death penalty on the grounds of insanity.

This led to a change in the legal attitude towards criminal responsibility. A Lord Chancellor at the end of the century, Farrer Herschell, 1st Baron Herschell, who served under Gladstone from 1892 to 1895 is remembered by **Herschell Street** in Anfield. Also in Anfield, there is a group of streets near Sleepers Hill named after politicians. Arthur Balfour, Prime Minister from 1902 to 1905 and earlier Lord Privy Seal is commemorated by **Balfour Street**. **Gorst Street** remembers Sir John Eldon Gorst, who was in government as Solicitor General and Vice President of the Committee on Education at the end of the 19th century. **Randolph Street** is after Lord Randolph Churchill, who had spells as Leader of the House of Commons, Chancellor of the Exchequer and Secretary of State for India. His son was wartime Prime Minister Sir Winston Churchill.

Brougham Terrace was the venue for many Liverpool marriages until the summer of 2000. This was named after Henry Peter Brougham, 1st Baron Brougham and Vaux (1778-1868). As a lawyer he defended Caroline of Brunswick against divorce proceedings brought against her by the Government (on behalf of George IV). He was elected to Parliament in 1810 and advocated liberal causes such as promotion of popular education. He was later Lord Chancellor from 1830 to 1834.

In Toxteth **Beaconsfield Street** commemorates Benjamin Disraeli, Earl of Beaconsfield who led the country from 1874 to 1880. Next to Beaconsfield Street is **Cairns Street**, named after Lord Cairns who Disraeli's Lord Chancellor. In another area of Toxteth, **Peel Street** was named after Sir Robert Peel, Prime Minister 1834-5 and 1841-6. He was founder of the modern Conservative Party as well as having been responsible for the introduction of a modern police force while he had been Home Secretary in 1829.

Further south, the centre of Garston can boast a cluster of streets named after Prime Ministers. In addition to **Gladstone Road Palmerston Road** (Viscount Palmerston PM 1855-65) and **Russell Road** (Earl Russell, PM 1865-6) are both named after Victorian leaders, with **Clarendon Road** being named after Lord Clarendon, Foreign Secretary in the 1850s. **Wellington Street** is named in honour of the Duke of Wellington, who went on to serve as Prime Minister on two separate occasions after his victory over Napoleon at Waterloo in 1815. His brother, Richard Colley Wellesley, 2nd Earl of Mornington is also remembered in Toxteth by **Mornington Street**. He served as Governor General of India from 1797 to 1805 and also as Foreign Minister from 1810 to 1812. **Granville Road** is named after George Leveson Gower, the 2nd Earl of Granville, who served as Foreign Secretary under both Russell and Gladstone. On the other side of the railway lines, Charles Hardinge, 1st Baron Hardinge of Penshurst, who was Viceroy of India from 1910 to 1916 has given his name to **Hardinge Road**.

Spencer Compton Cavendish, 8th Duke of Devonshire and Marquis of Hartington succeeded Gladstone as Liberal leader in 1875, only to hand the post back to him in 1880. **Cavendish Drive** in Walton and **Hartington Road** in Toxteth remember him. Spencer's father William Cavendish was also Earl of Burlington, giving his name to **Burlington Street** in Vauxhall. Going back even further, Spencer's grandfather, William George Cavendish was commemorated in Princes Park by **Devonshire Road** and **Devonshire Road West**. They were named as William's horticulturist Joseph Paxton designed the park. **Chatsworth Drive** in Edge Hill is named after the family's main residence, Chatsworth House in Derbyshire. Off Chatsworth Drive is **Ladybower Close**, named after the Ladybower Reservoir that was completed in 1943 in the Peak District. The reservoir is at the junction of the Derwent and Ashop rivers and its significance here is that the Derwent flows past Chatsworth House. The reservoir theme continued with **Redmires Close**, named after one in South Yorkshire.

A number of streets of Kensington are named after Lord Chancellors and senior judges from the late 19th and early 20th centuries. Two Lord Chancellors, Lord Cottenham and Lord Halsbury have given their names to **Cottenham Street** and **Halsbury Road**. **Denman Street,** as well as **Denman Drive** and **Denmam Road** in Newsham Park are named after Lord Chief Justice Thomas Denman. **Colebridge Street** remembers another Lord Chief Justice, John Coleridge 1st Baron Coleridge. The second most senior judge in England after the Lord Chief Justice is the Master of the Rolls, from where **Esher Street** has taken its name. William Brett, 1st Viscount Esher held this position from 1883 to 1897, serving under Coleridge.

John Bigham, 1st Viscount Mersey, had a brief spell in the 1890s as MP for Toxteth but it was in law where he excelled, being one of the richest barristers on the circuit. In 1912 he was appointed to head the inquiry on the British side of the Atlantic into the sinking of the Titanic. He is remembered by **Bigham Road**. Sir Robert Phillimore was an ecclesiastical and admiralty judge who is honoured by **Phillimore Road**. All these streets were so named due to their proximity to the judges' lodging in Newsham Park, where the travelling assize judges would reside while sitting in Liverpool. The Home Secretary between 1895 and 1900 when many of these judges were presiding was Matthew Ridley, 1st Viscount Ridley, after whom **Ridley Road** is named.

Heading out of Kensington in the direction of Old Swan, **Childers Street** remembers Hugh Childers, who was an unpopular Chancellor of the Exchequer with much of the public from 1882 to 1885 as he tried to raise income tax and alcohol duties. Charles Abbott, 1st Baron Abbott served as an interim Chancellor of the Exchequer in 1827 but his main contribution to politics was as the Lord Chief Justice from 1818 to 1832. **Tenterden Street** in Vauxhall is named after him.

More recently, wartime Premier Winston Churchill has been commemorated with **Churchill Way North & South**, the two flyovers which connect Commutation Row with Dale Street and Great Crosshall Street in the city centre. No local developer yet has dared name a street after Margaret Thatcher, the longest serving Prime Minister of the 20th century who made few friends on Merseyside. Neither have John Major, Tony Blair, Gordon Brown or David Cameron been commemorated. However, development by the Labour Council in the 1980s in Vauxhall did lead to a **Callaghan Close**, named after James Callaghan, Prime Minister from 1976 to 1979. When the street was developed, he was the most recent Labour Prime Minister and he is currently the most recent Prime Minister to be remembered in a Liverpool street.

Moving abroad, Italy was a group of separate states until 1871. One of the instrumental figures in unification was Giuseppe Mazzini, after whom **Mazzini Close**, which stands on the site of an earlier Mazzini Street in Everton, is named. Mazzini spent much of his time as an activist outside of the country and died just a year after seeing his wishes come true. 100,000 attended his funeral in Pisa.

ROYAL LIVERPOOL

J UST LIKE WITH POLITICIANS, earlier royals tend to be commemorated in central Liverpool while later ones are remembered elsewhere. The number of streets that a monarch had named after them does not necessarily correlate to how long was spent on the throne, as factors such as extent of development and popularity may have played a part.

The first monarch to be referred to in a street name in Liverpool was Queen Anne, who was on the throne from 1702-14. She gave her name to Queen Street, off Old Hall Street, although this is no longer in existence. However her husband, Prince George of Denmark's name lives on with **George Street** having been named after him. Both these streets were in existence on the first proper map of Liverpool, which was produced in 1725 by J Chadwick. There is also a **Queen Anne Street** off St Anne Street, which was developed at the end of the eighteenth century.

George I, who reigned from 1714 to 1727, was the first King of Britain to come from the House of Hanover. He never learnt the English language and usually conversed with his cabinet ministers in French. Frequent visits to Hanover meant he endeared himself little to the British public and as a consequence there are no streets in Liverpool named after him. His son George II, ruled from 1727 to 1760 and was the last British king to lead troops into battle, albeit Hanoverian ones in the War of the Austrian Succession. Despite his long reign there are no streets named after him, but both his sons are remembered. His younger son, William Duke of Cumberland, gave a Royal Inspection to Liverpool troops in 1746 after they helped defend Carlisle the year before during a Scottish rebellion. To commemorate this, **Hanover Street** was named after the ruling family's surname, while the old 'road to the quarry' became **Duke Street**. In addition to these two streets **Cumberland Street**, off Dale Street, was developed. George II's eldest son was Frederick Lewis, Prince of Wales, who is remembered by **Upper Frederick Street**. He died in 1751 while his father was still alive meaning he never became king and his son George took over as heir to the throne.

George III reigned for sixty years, from 1760 to 1820 and this coincided with Liverpool's rapid increase in development, which is reflected by the number of newly laid out streets that were named in his honour, making him by far the most represented sovereign in the city centre. With George Street already in existence, a fitting prefix was added when **Great George Street** was named, as his reign included several significant military victories. Initially called Great George's Street in the 1780s, it was joined by **Great George Place**. Around the time Great George Street was laid out, **Great Charlotte Street** and **Queen Square** were developed to commemorate his queen, Charlotte of Mecklenburg-Strelitz. There are two squares in different parts of the city centre named in connection with the king. **Great George Square** in Chinatown was meant to house an equestrian statue to commemorate his Golden Jubilee in 1810, but this project was cancelled due to lack of funds. Eventually, the statue was sited in **Monument Place**, the pedestrian area off London Road. As the docks system grew, George's (1771), Kings (1788) and Queens (1800) Docks all honoured George and Charlotte, giving rise to the current road names of **George's Dock Gates**, **Kings Parade**, **Kings Dock Road** and **Queens Wharf**.

Three of George III's seven children are commemorated in different parts of the city centre. **Cambridge Street**, **Clarence Street** and **York Street** are all named after the respective dukedoms of Adolphus, William (later William IV) and Frederick. Going even further, the extended family is remembered by **Brunswick Street**, after the family of which the Hanovers were a line. George III's nephew Prince William, Duke of gives his name to **Prince William Street** in Toxteth. In Wavertree there is a **Cambridge Street**, named after George III's grandson George William Frederick Charles, 2nd Duke of Cambridge, who was a commander in Crimea.

During the last ten years of his reign George III's mental illness, which he had suffered from for some time, became so severe that his eldest son, the future George IV, acted as Prince Regent. This fact was commemorated in **Regent Road**, commonly known as the 'dock road', as well as **Regent Street**. **Brunswick Road**, which links Everton Road and Islington, was developed in the early 1800s and named after Caroline of Brunswick, a member of his extended family who George had married in 1795. She gained a lot of sympathy from the British public after mistreatment from the new king, which included being denied access to their daughter and refused admission to his coronation in 1821. The queen also gave her name to Brunswick Dock, which is now served by **Brunswick Way**.

George IV was succeeded in 1830 by his brother William, Duke of Clarence, who had already been commemorated by Clarence Street. Despite only being on the throne for seven years, William IV made his mark with **William Henry Street** (Henry being his middle name) and **Upper William Street**. The latter was an extension of William Street, which is now called Cotton Street. **Adelaide Place** in Everton commemorates his wife Adelaide of Saxe-Meinengen. Also in Everton **Fitzclarence Way** has replaced an earlier Fitzclarence Street. This was re-named from Clarence Street when Everton was absorbed into Liverpool. The name Fitzclarence was given to the ten illegitimate children William had with actress Dorothea Jordan. One of these children, Elizabeth, was the great, great, great grandmother of David Cameron, who became Prime Minister in 2010.

Queen Victoria, nephew of William IV came to the throne at the age of eighteen in 1837, but is not greatly represented in the city centre as it had already become too clustered for further development by this time. However, slum clearance in the 1860s did enable the resulting new thoroughfare to be named **Victoria Street**. **Prince Albert Mews**, near Great George Street, remembers her husband Albert of Saxe-Coburg Gotha. His Germanic origins were recognised in the naming of Coburg Dock, which has subsequently given rise to the road of **Coburg Wharf**. Prince Albert also gave his name to Liverpool's first public park, Princes Park, which was opened in 1849. A boulevard style road was laid out to lead to it, which is flanked on either side by **Princes Avenue** and **Princes Road**.

Near to Prince Albert Mews, Victoria's second son Prince Alfred has given his name to **Alfred Mews**. This is a fairly recent development that takes its name from Alfred Street, which ran from Great George Street to the Anglican Cathedral but has now been demolished. Prince Alfred is also remembered in Wavertree, where he visited in 1866. To mark this, Cow Lane was re-named **Prince Alfred Road**, with a row of houses on it being named **Victoria Terrace**. Prince Alfred is also remembered in Wavertree, off Picton Road, by **Alfred Street.** Near to Prince Alfred Road is the **Victoria Park** private residential estate, where there is a **Victoria Avenue** and an **Albert Grove**. Albert Grove is off **Frederick Grove**, which commemorates the marriage of Princess Victoria, the first of Victoria and Albert's nine children, to

Frederick William, Crown Prince of Prussia. This cluster of streets is rounded off by **Arnold Grove**, which is named after Frieda Arnold, the Queen's dresser.

Off Smithdown Road **Avondale Road** is named after her grandson Albert Victor, Duke of Clarence and Avondale, who died in 1892 of influenza aged just 28. Two streets away **Claremont Road** takes its name from Claremont House in Esher, Surrey, which Victoria gave to her son Prince Leopold as a wedding present in 1882. Between Aigburth Road and Sefton Park, there is an **East**, **South** and **West Albert Road**, while Alexandra of Denmark (1844-1925), who married Victoria's eldest son Albert Edward (later Edward VII), in 1863 is commemorated by **Alexandra Drive**. Connecting Alexandra Drive to Aigburth Road is **Sandringham Drive**, named after Sandringham House in Norfolk, which was bought by Albert Edward in 1860 and was the birthplace of his son, the future George V. Albert Edward and Alexandra were popular figures who took on a lot of public duties after Queen Victoria became very introverted for some time following the death of her husband in 1861.

Off West Derby Road in Tuebrook are **Victoria Road** and **Albert Road**, which are joined by some streets named after their residences. **Buckingham Road** is named after Buckingham Palace, which was purchased by the Royal Family in 1761 but did not become the monarch's main residence until Victoria's reign. **Osborne Road** remembers Osborne House, built between 1845 and 1851 by Victoria and Albert as a holiday home. This palace, on the Isle of Wight, is where Victoria died in 1901. Like in Aigburth, Sandringham House is commemorated, this time by **Sandringham Road**, while **Marlborough Road** takes its name from the London royal residence of Marlborough House, which was occupied by Edward VII before he became king. It is now used as offices of the Commonwealth Secretariat. **Windsor Road** is named after Windsor Castle, which was founded by William the Conqueror in the 11th century.

In Orrell Park there are the familiar names of **Albert Drive** and **Victoria Drive.** Nearby, royal residences are again remembered by **Buckingham Road** and **Windsor Road**, as well as **Balmoral Road**, named after Balmoral Castle in Aberdeenshire, purchased by Prince Albert in 1852. **Chelsea Road** takes its name not from Queen Victoria's favourite football team, but from the location of the Royal Hospital, opened at the end of the 17th century for retired and injured soldiers. Its residents are more commonly known as the Chelsea Pensioners and the Chelsea Flower Show takes place in its grounds every year. Other streets with a royal theme in this area are **Palace Road** and **Regina Road**, Regina being the Latin word for queen. Off Warbreck Moor stands **Eastbourne Road**, which is named after Victoria's favourite holiday resort and **Albany Road**, after her son Prince Leopold, Duke of Albany. Near the Breeze Hill flyover, two more of their children are honoured. **Arthur Street** is named after the couple's third son Arthur (1850-1942), while his sister Helena (1846-1923) was their third daughter, giving her name to **Helena Street**. Other streets around Liverpool to be named with Victorian connections include **Queens Road** in Everton, which was developed while Victoria was on the throne and **Albert Street** and **Helena Street** in Edge Hill. There is also an **Empress Road** in Cabbage Hall, which recognises Victoria's position of Empress of India.

Perhaps the most interesting of all streets named in relation to Queen Victoria are to be found in a cluster between Hall Lane and Kensington. These streets were laid out after Victoria's Golden Jubilee in 1887 and the theme includes members of her extended family. Victoria is directly commemorated by **Empress Road**, as is the jubilee itself in **Jubilee Drive**. **Albert Edward Road** and **Renfrew Road** remember the heir to the throne, Baron Renfrew being a title given to him under Scottish peerage. **Leopold Road** and **Albany Road** commemorate his brother Leopold, duke of Albany, while **Connaught Road** is named after Prince Arthur, Duke of Connaught. Albert and Victoria's Germanic connections are remembered in **Saxony Road** and **Guelph Street**, with the Guelphs being a family of which they were a branch line. **Battenberg Street** remembers Prince Henry of Battenberg, who married Princess Beatrice, while **Teck Street** is named after Mary of Teck, who married Victoria's grandson George Duke of York in 1893. She would later be better known as Queen Mary when George became George V.

One street with connections to Queen Victoria that stands alone is **Frogmore Road**, off Prescot Road, which is named after the Frogmore mausoleum, where Victoria and Albert are buried. This is situated in the grounds surrounding Windsor Castle and although a crypt with nine spaces for each of their children was built, none of them chose to be buried there.

Edward VII, son of Queen Victoria was sixty when he came to the throne and only reigned for nine years. **King Edward Street**, linking Great Howard Street with New Quay was named after him while in Edge Hill and Wavertree, his wife is honoured by two streets both named **Alexandra Road**. The street in Edge Hill is the sole survivor of a group of streets to honour Alexandra, her homeland having also been commemorated here by the now demolished Copenhagen Road and Denmark Road. George V reigned from 1910 to 1936. No streets are named after him, but near to Alexandra Road in Wavertree is **Augusta Close.** This is a relatively new development replacing an earlier Augusta Street and named after his wife Victoria Mary Augusta, who was more commonly known as Queen Mary. Like Teck Street, this had been named before she became queen.

Queens Drive was developed as Liverpool's second ring road between 1903 and 1912, during which time both Alexandra and Mary were queen. In 1922 Princess Mary, daughter of George V and Queen Mary, married Viscount Lascelles and to honour this event **Lascelles Road** on the Springwood Estate in Allerton was named. This runs off **Stamfordham Drive**, named after Arthur Bigge, Baron Stamfordham who was Private Secretary to George V. He was very influential, persuading him to change the Royal Family's surname to Windsor from Saxe-Coburg Gotha in light of the outbreak of the 1st World War.

King George VI, who was on the throne from 1936 to 1952, is not commemorated in name by any streets in Liverpool but **Kingsdale Road** and **Queensdale Road** in Mossley Hill were developed during his reign. Queensdale Road refers to Queen Elizabeth, the Queen Mother who celebrated her 100th birthday in 2000 and died in March 2002. It is a sign of changing attitudes towards the royal family that no streets within the city of Liverpool boundary have been named in relation to Queen Elizabeth II, despite her having reigned since 1952. However, there have been some streets named after her in Huyton and Widnes.

MILITARY LIVERPOOL

FAMOUS BATTLES, wars and military leaders have long been a major factor in the naming of streets in Liverpool. Again the expansion of the city over time can be seen in the fact that, generally speaking, the more central the street, the longer ago the event that named it took place. However, there are some exceptions to this rule.

In Allerton, **Archerfield Road** is named after the Robin Hood Stone, which was moved to its present location on the corner with Booker Avenue in 1928, after having stood near Greenwood Road for centuries. The stone is said to have been used by archers in the reign of Henry VIII (1509-47) to sharpen their arrows.

During the English Civil War (1642-6), Prince Rupert used the village of Everton, which provided a clear vantage point of Liverpool, to launch his attack on the town. Redevelopment has seen that Rupert Lane, Rupert Terrace, Prince Rupert Street, Rupert Hill and Rupert Grove, which were once all in the Village Street vicinity, have long since disappeared. For the last quarter of the 20th century, the only reminder left was the Rupert Lane Recreation Ground, but the newly created **Rupert Drive** has redressed this balance partly of late.

In Walton, some streets around the village centre were named some 300+ years after the Civil War. An act that eventually led to the Civil War was the refusal by some statesmen to pay ship money, a tax levied by King Charles I for the Royal Navy. Two of these, John Hampden and John Pym, are remembered in **Hampden Street** and **Pym Street**. John Lenthall, who had been the Speaker of Parliament when it rebelled against the King, is commemorated by **Lenthall Street**, **Mandeville Street** is named after Edward Montagu, Viscount Mandeville who commanded Parliament's Eastern Association army. The war was ended in England when Charles I was defeated at Naseby in 1645 and fled to Scotland, giving rise to the name **Naseby Street**. A key battle that occurred in Scotland was in 1650 at Dunbar, when Parliamentarian forces defeated Scots loyal to the King, hence **Dunbar Street**. Following the end of the war, the first commoner to rule England was Oliver Cromwell, after whom **Cromwell Street** is named. His son-in-law Henry Ireton, who was a signatory on the king's death warrant, gives his name to **Ireton Street**.

Sedgemoor Road in Norris Green is named after the last battle to take place on English soil. This occurred in 1685 at Sedgemoor in Somerset when James Scott, Duke of Monmouth and illegitimate son of Charles II tried to claim the Crown after the death of his father. Forces representing his uncle, James II, who Charles had nominated to be King before he died, defeated him. In the battle Monmouth was captured and he was later executed for treason.

The Battle of the Boyne was fought in Ireland in 1690 and saw William III defeat James II, who he had deposed as King two years earlier. The victory ended James' hopes of regaining the throne and was a step towards securing English rule in Ireland, the battle is still commemorated today every 12th of July by Protestants. One of William's commanders was a German, Meinhardt Schomberg, 1st Duke Schomberg, after whom **Schomberg Street** in Kensington is named.

In 1692 Admiral Edward Russell was in charge of a combined British and Dutch fleet, which defeated a French invasion fleet at the bay of La Hogue on the northern coast of France. **Russell Street** in the city centre remembers him.

The War of the Spanish Succession (1701-14) was fought by England, Austria, Netherlands and Denmark against France and Spain. Commander in Chief of the English forces was John Churchill and his victory against the French at Blenheim in 1704 saw the beginning of the decline of French dominance in Europe. Further victories at Ramillies in 1706 and Oudenarde in 1708 saw him given the title 1st Duke of Marlborough. He gives his name to **Marlborough Street**, although this was not named until the end of the 18th century sometime after his victories

Off Penny Lane in Wavertree, two of Churchill's victories are remembered by **Blenheim Road** and **Ramillies Road**, both developed in the 20th century. Also in this vicinity, **Balcarres Avenue** remembers Alexander Lindsay, the 4th Earl of Balcarres who was a captain during this Flanders campaign, while **Crawford Avenue** is in relation to the fact that the earldoms of Balcarres and Crawford were merged in 1848. James Butler, 2nd Duke of Ormond (1665-1745), succeeded Marlborough as Commander in Chief of the British forces in 1711, having already served Queen Anne as Lord Lieutenant of Ireland. He was remembered by **Ormond Street**, which was developed shortly after the end of the war off Old Hall Street.

In 1715 John Campbell, 2nd Duke of Argyll, suppressed a Scottish rebellion. He had fought under Marlborough at Malplaquet in 1709 and also played a key part in the opening of negotiations for the Union of England and Scotland, which took place in 1707. **Argyle Street**, which runs parallel to the bottom of Duke Street off Paradise Street, is named after him.

The last British King to participate in Battle was George II, at Dettingen, Bavaria in 1743. George, who was also elector of Hanover, subordinated British interests to take part in the War of the Austrian Succession (1740-8), against an alliance that included France, Prussia and Spain. **Anson Place** and **Anson Street** are named after Admiral George Anson, who was made a Baronet after defeating the French at Cape Finisterre in 1747. During the first four years of the war, he circumnavigated the globe preying on Spanish colonies and ships, bringing back a fortune in treasure. Unusually **Fontenoy Street** remembers a battle that was lost. In 1745 at the Battle of Fontenoy in Belgium the French beat British, Austrian and Dutch forces.

The Seven Years War of 1756-63 saw Britain line up alongside Hanover and Prussia against Austria, France, Russia, Spain and Sweden for control of Germany and colonial supremacy in North America and India. The Prussian alliance was commemorated by **Prussia Street**, which once ran from Old Hall Street to Pall Mall and beyond but was cut in two by the building of Exchange Station, now the Mercury Court office complex. Admiral Edward Hawke, after whom **Hawke Street** is named, won the Battle of Quiberon Bay off the coast of Brittany in 1759, thwarting a planned French invasion of England. James Wolfe was Britain's second in command in North America and gives his name to **Wolfe Street** in Toxteth. He was killed in battle while taking Quebec from the French in 1759.

Three years after the Seven Years War ended, in 1766, a French invasion was threatened. Gill Slater, remembered by **Slater Street** and **Slater Place**, commanded the Liverpool Volunteers, a citizens regiment of volunteer soldiers which was raised in response to this.

Another local man who would raise an army at his own expense was Colonel John Bolton, who gathered 800 local men in 1797 when the French tried to invade Wales. Bolton lived in Duke Street and in 1805 he fought and won the last duel to be fought in Liverpool. Although charged with murder, he was saved by the weight of public opinion in his favour and never stood trial. He is honoured in Liverpool by **Bolton Street**.

During the last third of the 18th century a number of colonial battles were fought as Britain held on to colonies and fought off the threat of other powers that tried to exert a naval influence. In 1782, French hopes for supremacy in the West Indies were ended by a three day battle off Dominica. Under the command of Admiral George Brydges, the French commander Francois de Grasse was captured along with seven of his ships. Brydges was given the title of 1ˢᵗ Baron Rodney for this victory and in Liverpool the proposed name for Schlink Street, after a Dutch local landowner, was changed to **Rodney Street**. On his return to England, Rodney was a champion of the slave trade and spoke against its abolition in the House of Lords. Another Rodney Street was developed in Toxteth, but to avoid confusion this was later changed to its present title of **Admiral Street**, with an **Admiral Grove** also being present nearby. He is also commemorated by **Brydges Street** in Edge Hill.

Britain had taken possession of the rock of Gibraltar in 1704, during the War of the Spanish Succession. When Spain entered the War of American Independence against the British it laid siege to the colony from 1779 to 1783, only ending it when peace preliminaries were signed. **Gibraltar Row** commemorates this and there was once a Gibraltar Street. **Elliot Street**, which was opened up in 1822 as an entrance to Clayton Square after the closure of the roperies for the development of St. Johns Market, is named after George Augustus Elliot, one of the British defenders of the siege.

The threat of Dutch naval superiority over Britain was ended in 1797 by victory over Admiral de Winter at Camperdown, off the Dutch coast. Under the command of Admiral Adam Duncan, the Dutch fleet was destroyed and **Duncan Street** was named in his honour. Also in 1797 the French fleet were defeated at Cape St Vincent, off Portugal. The commander, Admiral John Jervis (1735-1823) was made 1st Earl of St. Vincent and **St. Vincent Street** was laid out in the early 19th century. **St. Vincent Way**, developed later, is also present.

The Napoleonic Wars, fought between France and a number of European powers from 1799 to 1815 saw a number of significant military victories on land and sea. The main naval hero of the wars was Horatio Nelson, who was already a distinguished commander, having won earlier battles against the French before key victories at Copenhagen in 1801 and Trafalgar in 1805. At Copenhagen he destroyed the Danish fleet, which was giving economic aid to France. Already having lost an eye and arm in battle, he was then mortally wounded at Trafalgar, a victory that put paid to Napoleon's plans to invade England. In the city centre, **Nelson Street** and **Lord Nelson Street** are both named after him. His Flag Captain, Lieutenant Thomas Masterman Hardy (1769-1839) is remembered by **Hardy Street**, which runs parallel to Nelson Street. Hardy commanded HMS Victory at Trafalgar and was at Nelson's side as he died. Off Brunswick Road, **Trafalgar Way** remembers Nelson's final battle. **Mansfield Street** in Everton is named after Captain Charles John Moore Mansfield, who fought at both Copenhagen and Trafalgar, taking 25 prisoners and capturing a ship in the latter.

Admiral William Hotham (1736-1813) and Admiral Alexander Hood, Lord Bridport (1726-1814) both commanded Nelson in his earlier years in the navy. **Hotham Street**, which was originally called Duncan Street and linked Copperas Hill with London Road prior to the building of Lime Street station, is named in Hotham's honour. Off Hotham Street is **Bridport Street**, which remembers Hood who served in the navy for 54 years, still commanding at the age of 74.

A less famous commander than Nelson was Admiral James Gambier. Before being put in charge of the Channel fleet from 1808 to 1811 he was involved in a bombardment of Copenhagen in 1807. His actions in the Napoleonic Wars led to him being appointed Governor of Newfoundland in Canada. In Liverpool **Gambier Terrace**, which was developed in the 1830s and overlooks the Anglican Cathedral, honours him. When Napoleon was transported to exile at St. Helena in 1815 the commander of the ship that carried him was Sir George Cockburn (1772-1853). He had served under Nelson in the Mediterranean from 1795 to 1797 and is remembered in Toxteth by **Cockburn Street**.

The Napoleonic wars eventually ended in 1815 when French leader Napoleon Bonaparte was defeated in the land Battle of Waterloo in Belgium, an event that was commemorated when **Waterloo Road** was developed. The battle also gave the name to Waterloo Dock and the road around it, **Waterloo Quay**. There is also a **Waterloo Street** in Wavertree. Arthur Wellesley, Duke of Wellington was in command of the Allied armies at Waterloo, but considering how successful he was in military terms, **Wellington Street**, north of the city centre is very low key. Throughout the city however, he has more streets named after him than any other military figure, of which **Wellington Road** in Wavertree is a main route. There is another Wellington Road in Toxteth, where **Wellesley Road** and **Wellesley Terrace** remember his real surname. **Orthes Street** was named after the Battle of Orthes, in southern France in 1814, where an Anglo Portuguese army led by Wellington defeated French troops.

In Everton, **Douro Street** commemorates the Battle of Douro in 1809, in which Wellington took control of the Portuguese city of Porto. One of his generals during this battle was William Carr Beresford, 1st Viscount Beresford, after whom nearby **Beresford Street** was named. There is also a **Beresford Road** in Toxteth, near to Wellington Road. It was not just Europe where Napoleon was fought. Sir Ralph Abercromby (1734-1801), after whom **Abercromby Square** is named, was killed in the Battle of Alexandria, which saw the Egyptian city given back to the Turks following a British attack on the occupying French forces.

Although there were many important victories during George III's reign, it was not always successful, as he ruled over Britain's loss of America as a colony during the American War of Independence (1775-83). One member of the Tarleton family, after whom **Tarleton Street** is named (see slave traders), was Banastre (1754-1833), a British commander who distinguished himself at Waxhaw Creek in South Carolina, earning himself the nickname 'Bloody Tarleton'. Banastre himself was commemorated by Banastre Street, which once stood on the site of the Kingsway Tunnel entrance. However, **Blackstock Street** survives, commemorating the Battle of Blackstock's Farm in South Carolina in 1780. In this battle an army commanded by Tarleton was outnumbered by four to one and lost nearly half of its men, although he was able to claim some success in wounding the American commander, Thomas Sumter. He had sailed to America with Charles Cornwallis, who gives his name to **Cornwallis Street**. It was his surrender at Yorktown in 1781 that helped ensure American victory, but he later negotiated the Treaty of Amiens in 1802 that ended one phase of the Napoleonic Wars.

By the mid 19th century, most of the main streets in the city centre as we know it today were in place, meaning later military campaigns were remembered further afield. For instance, the Crimean War, which was fought between Britain, France and Turkey against Russia between 1853 and 1856, is commemorated in Garston, Aigburth and Wavertree. **Raglan Street** and **Raglan Walk** in Garston are named after Fitzroy James Henry Somerset, 1st Baron Raglan. He was an aide-de-camp (someone who offers administrative support) to the Duke of Wellington at Waterloo, before going on to command British forces in Crimea where he died of dysentery. A key victory in the Crimean War was the battle for the Alma River and **Alma Road** in Aigburth and **Alma Terrace** in Wavertree remember this.

Florence Nightingale became famous for her treatment of wounded soldiers during the Crimea War. However when she chose her party of 38 to travel there she omitted to take Mary Seacole, a Jamaican who had come to London offering her experience of treating tropical diseases. Undeterred Mary borrowed funds herself and travelled there, opening a hotel where sick people could call in and visiting battlefields to treat the wounded. For many years after her death her work went unnoticed but over the last twenty years she has been getting the recognition she deserves and was voted 1st place in an online poll for the Greatest 100 Black Britons in 2004. The same year, off Lodge Lane, **Seacole Close** was developed.

Guns made at the Fawcett Preston foundry of Duke Street were used in the American Civil War (1861-5). Initially this was called the Phoenix Foundry and **Lydia Ann Street**, which led to it, was named after the wife of its founder George Perry. The last act of the American Civil War also took place in Liverpool, when the Confederate ship CSS Shenandoah surrendered in the River Mersey, the captain not docking in the US as he faced execution. The ship was then docked at Herculaneum Dock, which was built on the site of the former Herculaneum Pottery Company in Toxteth. This was in existence from 1796 to 1833 before they were forced to fold due to the level of competition from Staffordshire. The dock has given the name to **Herculaneum Court** and **Herculaneum Road**, while **Charleston Road** commemorates the South Carolina city with which Liverpool had close links during the civil war and rest of the 19th century, importing a large quantity of cotton from there.

In 1867 Thoedore II of Abyssinia (now Ethiopia) imprisoned the British consul and other Europeans after Britain rebuked his efforts to form an alliance. An invasion force was sent and the fall of the fortress of Magdala led to Theodore committing suicide rather than face capture. **Magdala Street** in Toxteth commemorates this, while **Abyssinia Close** in Wavertree, which has replaced an earlier Abyssinia Street, remembers the campaign as a whole.

A **Bosnia Street** exists in Toxteth, although it was not named in relation to events of the 1990s. This street was in existence over 100 years earlier following the Congress of Berlin in 1878, which saw the ex-Turkish province of Bosnia mandated to Austria-Hungary following Russia's victory over the Turks. Britain was a major player in the Congress, due to its concern over Russia's growing military strength. Two other streets named at the same time - Balkan Street and a Plevna Street, have now been swept away by redevelopment.

In Wavertree around Picton Road and Lawrence Road there are some streets named in relation to the Boer War, fought between British and Dutch settlers between 1899 and 1902. **Wauchope Street** remembers Albert Gilbert Wauchope, a commander killed during the Battle of Magersfontein in December 1899. Wauchope had been serving under Field Marshal Paul Sanford Methuen, 3rd Baron Methuen, after whom **Methuen Street** is named. He went on to become the only British general captured during the Boer War in 1902 and after hostilities ended returned to South Africa to govern Natal. Sir Archibald Hector MacDonald, who gave his name to **Macdonald Street**, was knighted for his Boer War service, playing a key part in operations in Bloemfontein, Pretoria and Paardeberg. He would go on to commit suicide in 1903, before he was due to face a court martial concerning sexual liaisons with boys in Ceylon.

Plumer Street is named after Herbert Plumer, who was involved in the relieving the Siege of Mafeking in 1900. He went on to be a Field Marshal on the Western Front in the 1st World War. Another commander remembered by **Broadwood Road** is Robert George Broadwood, **Strathcona Road** commemorates the Strahcona's horse regiment, recruited in 1901 from Canada at the expense of Lord Strathcona. The regiment arrived in Cape Town in April of that year and were renowned for their scouting skills.

In the north end of the city there is a cluster of Boer War themed streets in Fazakerley. **Ladysmith Road** is named after the siege of the railway town of Ladysmith, while **Delagoa Road** is named after Delagoa Bay, an important seaport during the war. The town of Harrismith was a major British base and is remembered by **Harrismith Road**. **Redvers Drive** and **Kitchener Drive** in Orrell Park are named after Boer War commanders Sir Redvers Buller and Horatio Kitchener. Kitchener would become most famous for his role in the 1st World War, when as Secretary of State for War he appeared on the poster stating 'Your Country Needs You'. He drowned in 1916 after a ship he was travelling to Russia on was hit by a German missile.

The biggest group of streets relating to the 1st World War (1914-18) spans Queens Drive in the Tuebrook/Clubmoor area, with more than a dozen streets having connections. **Culme Road** remembers Vice Admiral Sir Michael Culme Seymour, a commander in the Battle of Jutland. Running off this is **Halsey Crescent** and **Halsey Avenue**, after Sir Lionel Halsey who also commanded a vessel at Jutland and was in 1918 appointed Commander in Chief of the Australian Navy. Another Australian is remembered by **Birdwood Road**. Sir William Birdwood was commander of the Australian and New Zealand Corps (ANZACs) for most of the 1st World War. He was succeeded by Sir John Monash in 1918, after whom **Monash Road** is named.

Cavan Road was named after Frederick Lambart, the Earl of Cavan who had retired from military service in 1913. However after the outbreak of war he was recalled from the reserve and went on to become Commander in Chief of British forces on the Italian front. Running off Cavan Road is **Wapshare Road**, which takes its name from Brigadier R Wapshare, a commander in the British Indian Army in Mesopotamia, modern day Iraq.

Aside from commanders, a number of recipients of the Victoria Cross have also been honoured in this area. **Tollerton Road** is named after Ross Tollerton, who carried a wounded soldier back to safety in Aisne northern France in 1914. William Angus, who gives his name to **Angus Road**, received his Victoria Cross for the same act, rescuing a wounded soldier from within yards of enemy lines at Givenchy. Another Givenchy recipient was James Hewitson, who fought off a machine gun team coming towards him in 1918, capturing one and killing ten. **Hewiston Road** and **Hewitson Avenue** are named after him.

Edward Bellew, after whom **Bellew Road** is named, was a Canadian who fought single handed against the Germans at Ypres to try and fend off an attack after his regiment suffered heavy losses. When his ammunition ran out he was captured and remained a prisoner for the rest of the war. His second cousin, Robert Bellew Adams, had already received a Victoria Cross in the Boer War. An Australian, Lieutenant Albert Borella, gave his name to **Borella Road**. He led his platoon to safety from enemy lines in 1918 after capturing some German gunners. Off Borella Road is **Maxwell Road**, named after compatriot Joseph Maxwell who captured a machine gun from behind German barbed wire lines in 1918. Another Australian was Albert Lowerson, who captured fifty prisoners and twelve machine guns at Mont St Quentin in 1918, an act commemorated by **Lowerson Road.**

Augustus Agar, remembered by **Agar Road** was a naval officer at Gallipoli and then off the coast of northern Russia. He was awarded the Victoria Cross in 1919 for his work ferrying British agents out of Russia, which had become Communist in 1917. The Victoria Cross recipients honoured in this area mentioned so far survived the war, but many others were not so lucky and received their awards posthumously having made the ultimate sacrifice during their heroic deeds. One of those was John Liddell, after whom **Liddell Road** is named. He died in Belgium in 1915 after the plane he was piloting was shot at. However before he died he still managed to get the aircraft back to Allied lines safely, saving the life of his fellow crew member.

The 1st World War is also commemorated by a small cluster of streets off St Oswald's Street in Old Swan. The longest of the roads is **Davidson Road**, which carries a local connection. Sir Jonathan Roberts Davidson, who as a commander in the Liverpool Scottish was twice wounded on the Western Front along with Noel Chevasse, who would go on to receive a Victoria Cross for rescuing fellow wounded soldiers. After the war Davidson became the city of Liverpool's Chief Engineer. **Allenby Square** is named after Edward Allenby who led the offensive against the Turks, capturing Damascus and Jerusalem, while **Rawlinson Road** commemorates Sir Henry Rawlinson, who played a major role in the Battle of the Somme. A naval commander, David Beatty is remembered by **Beatty Road**. He played a part in the Battle of Jutland in 1916, when the Allied naval blockade of Germany was maintained, despite the German fleet being of greater numbers. Finally, **Dorien Road**, which contains a slight misspelling, takes its name from Sir Horace Smith-Dorrien, who commanded troops on the Western Front at Mons and Ypres.

Fazakerley also commemorates the 1st World War in addition to the Boer War. **Karonga Road** is named after the site of a battle in Malawi that was fought against forces from German East Africa. **Manica Crescent** remembers HMS Manica, a kite balloon ship that was used at Gallipoli, when allied forces unsuccessfully tried to invade Turkey to re-take Istanbul.

Not far from St Oswald's Street, off Edge Lane Drive, is **Sturdee Road**, named after Admiral Sir Charles Doveton Sturdee, whose victory in the Battle of the Falklands in 1914 gave Britain control of the ocean trade routes. On the same estate as Sturdee Road, **Robeck Road** commemorates Admiral Sir John Michael de Robeck, who oversaw the evacuation of Gallipoli in 1915 after his attempt to take it had failed and he refused to try again in case there were further heavy losses. He then took command of the Grand Fleet, which protected Britain's shores.

In Childwall there is a **Givenchy Close**, named after the site of the Spring 1918 German offensive. The British 55th division, containing many Liverpool territorials, was commanded by Major General Hugh Sandham Jeudwine, who managed to fend off the offensive and keep the channel ports in allied hands. **Jeudwine Close** in Woolton remembers him. Near to here, **Cavell Close** is named after Edith Cavell, a British nurse who ran a clinic in occupied Brussels during the 1st World War and was shot by the Germans for treason after helping allied soldiers escape to Holland.

In 1995, to commemorate the 50th anniversary of the Battle of the Atlantic, which was fought from 1940 to 1944, **Canada Boulevard** was created in front of the three main waterfront buildings. This honoured Canada's involvement in the naval battle, which was co-ordinated from Liverpool. Canadian maple trees were planted but unfortunately they didn't suit the British climate and have since been replaced with Norwegian ones. As with royalty, more recent conflicts have not been remembered within the city boundary, despite the large-scale building programmes that went on in the 1950s. The nearest group of World War Two linked streets is in Huyton.

The Falklands Conflict of 1982 has been remembered on the Gillmoss Industrial Estate by way of ships that were involved. **Hermes Road** was named after the aircraft carrier HMS *Hermes*, the flagship of the British fleet during the conflict, which set sail for the South Atlantic just three days after the Argentine invasion. *Hermes* was joined by HMS *Invincible*, which gives its name to **Invincible Way**. As well as the Falklands, *Invincible* was also used in conflicts in the 1990s against Iraq and Yugoslavia before being decommissioned in 2005 and sold to a Turkish ship recycling company in 2011. The third street, **Canberra Lane**, is named after a civilian vessel, P & O cruise ship SS *Canberra* which was commandeered by the Ministry of Defence to transport ground troops to the conflict.

After Deysbrook Army Barracks in West Derby closed in 2002 a supermarket and housing was built on the site. The old army barracks have been remembered by the army ranks of **Brigadier Drive**, **Cadet Way** and **Colonel Drive**.

84

LIVERPOOL'S LUNGS – BOTANICAL GARDENS & 19TH CENTURY PARKS

D URING THE LATE 19TH CENTURY it became apparent that Liverpool's residents needed somewhere they could go to escape the increasing overcrowding and pollution in the town. The answer lay in the botanical gardens and parks, which provided an oasis of calm for town dwellers and in the case of botanical gardens, the opportunity to see plants that were native to other lands.

The first botanical gardens was opened in 1802 in Olive Street, which was situated off Crown Street. As the surrounding area became more built up over the next few decades, many of the newly laid out streets were named with a botanical theme and remain in existence today. Major routes are **Grove Street** and **Myrtle Street**, the myrtle being a tree/shrub found in tropical America and Asia. Another street named after a plant from the Tropics is **Mulberry Street**, while **Peach Street** and **Walnut Street** have just about survived total obliteration by the University of Liverpool, remaining as pedestrian throughways in the campus.

The botanical gardens remained in Grove Street until 1836, when the expanding town meant it was necessary for them to move to a site off Edge Lane, which was then a rural area. The land south of the new gardens was originally meant to be a gaol, but when this idea was deemed impractical it was developed into Wavertree Park in 1856. This is now known as Botanic Park and the original site of the walled gardens is still intact and in use as part of the park. **Botanic Road**, which runs alongside the park, was named in honour of the gardens. Terraced property began to engulf this area in the 1860s and a number of new roads laid out between Edge Lane and Prescot Road continued the naming precedent set by streets around the first gardens in the city centre. These included **Laburnum Road**, **Laurel Road** and **Lilley Road**.

Today, the botanical gardens are situated in Calderstones Park, one of several public parks in the city. It was realised in the 19th century that there was a need for open spaces where residents could exercise because although there was St James Walk on the site of the Anglican Cathedral, this was still near to the fumes from the docks. Princes Park was the first public park to be developed in 1849 and in the 1860s the corporation decided to build three large parks in the south, middle and north of the city. These were Sefton Park, Newsham Park and Stanley Park.

Around the perimeter of Princes Park, land was sold for the building of upper class residences so that the development costs of the park could be recouped in ground rent. One of the roads developed was **Belvidere Road**, which was named as a compliment to the Classical style of the houses, a belvedere being a detached structure built to command a view. The word comes from two Italian words meaning beautiful and to see. Interestingly, it is actually mis-spelled; Belvedere, as in the school, is the correct way. **Ullett Road** separates Princes Park from the much larger Sefton Park. This name derives from owlet and the section between Sefton Park Road and Smithdown Road was in existence in the 18th century as Owlet Lane. Two roads, **Livingston Drive North** and **Livingston Drive South** were laid out to connect Sefton Park with Lark Lane and Aigburth Road respectively. They were named after Joseph G. Livingston, from whom the land was bought to provide the approaches.

In Newsham Park there is an **Orphan Drive**. This was named after the Royal Liverpool Seamen's Orphan Institution, which was in existence from 1864 to 1949 in the building that became Park Hospital but has sadly been in a derelict state since 2004.

Throughout Liverpool, there are reminders of greener pastures in the names of many streets. Builders may have been hoping residents would re-create a rural air in their imagination, but an article in the *Liverpool Citizen* of 1890 suggested that some of these should be renamed, as they did nothing to reflect their surroundings. The writer may have been referring to **Moss Grove** and **Fern Grove** in Toxteth, or **Crocus Street** and **Snowdrop Street** in Kirkdale, which were far from the countryside when developed. The names have survived however and there are many more modern developments that have continued to give rise to botanical names. One example is **Lavender Way**, near Walton Park. Roads off this are **Buttercup Way**, **Dahlia Close**, **Honeysuckle Drive** and **Limetree Close**. In Croxteth Park, **Fir Tree Drive** rings the estate, which includes roads such as **Elm Close**, **The Cedars** and **The Oaks**.

THE WELSH & SCOTTISH
INFLUENCE

T HE WELSH and Scottish influence in Liverpool can be seen by
a number of streets around the city, although the Welsh were
more prominent. Streets developed by builders would often
remember their homelands and in some cases leave residents quite
tongue twisted!

In the mid to late 19th century, there were a number of Welsh building
societies, estate agents and builders in Liverpool. One famous builder
was John Jones, nicknamed 'Drinkwater' because of his refusal to pay
workmen the customary price of a pint of beer when the first house in
a terrace was completed. Another was William Jones, the first Welsh-
speaking mayor of Bootle who built streets in Everton and Toxteth.

Off High Park Street in Toxteth, **Dovey Street**, **Elwy Street** and
Gwydir Street are all named after Welsh rivers, with Kinmel Bay
giving its name to **Kinmel Street**. **Madryn Street** and **Powis Street**
are named after castles in Gwynedd and Powys respectively, although
Madryn Castle was demolished in 1968 and is now a caravan park.
Pengwern Street, **Rhiwlas Street** and **Wynnstay Street** take their
names from villages while **Voelas Street** is named after a country
house estate in the Vale of Conwy. **Teilo Street** is named after a
6th century Welsh saint who allegedly accompanied St. David on a
pilgrimage to Jerusalem. A smaller number of Welsh streets can be
found on the other side of Park Road, off Park Street. Here, **Rhyl
Street** is named after the north Welsh coastal resort, while **Llanwryst
Close** has replaced the earlier Llanwryst Street. This was named after
the town of Llanwryst, which like the Voelas Estate is in the Vale of
Conwy.

In Vauxhall, around the Athol Street and Boundary Street area, a
number of terraced streets were developed with Welsh connections.
Most of these have been cleared, but some street names do survive.
Amongst those still present are **Denbigh Street** and **Milford Street**,
which are named after towns. **Barmouth Way** and **Newport Court**
are both newly created, using names from streets that were first

developed years before. Extensive re-development has occurred around Breck Road and Everton Road, but a Welsh name that lives on is **Aber Street**, named after a village near Bangor. **Fishguard Close** remembers an earlier street that was named after a port in south west Wales, while **Lavan Street** and the newer **Lavan Close** are named after the Lavan Sands in north west Wales.

Off Walton Breck Road, a Free Welsh Church was established at the corner of Donaldson Street and Glaisher Street, which still stands as Crete Hall. In the immediate vicinity is **Tenby Street**, which is named after a town in south Wales. Nearby is **Vrynwy Street**, which takes its name from Lake Vrynwy, Liverpool's main water supply since the 1880s when a reservoir was constructed there. Off Oakfield Road, **Bala Street** is also named after a lake, while **Dinorwic Road** and **Valley Road** are named after villages in Gwynedd and Anglesey respectively. **Skerries Road** takes its name from a small group of uninhabited islands off the north western Anglesey coast. Amongst these streets named after Welsh places are a number which were given girls names. They are **Wylva Road**, **Edith Road**, **Miriam Road**, **Gertrude Road**, **Elsie Road** and **Lilian Road**. It may be that they were names of family members of the builder. One street on the edge of the city centre that definitely was named after family connections was **Catharine Street**. This was developed in 1848 by William Jones and named after his mother, with one of the houses being built specially for her.

A family firm of builders, 'Owen and William Owen Elias', who were father and son, built streets in Walton that spelt out the name of their firm in alphabetical order. Between County Road and Goodison Road, running in this order are **O**xton, **W**inslow, **E**ton, **N**eston, **A**ndrew, **N**imrod, **D**ane, **W**ilburn, **I**smay, **L**ind, **L**owell, **I**ndex and **A**rnot Streets. The sequence continues on the other side of County Road with **M**akin, **O**lney, **W**eldon, **E**uston and **N**ixon Streets. Over Bedford Road, the sequence is reversed to complete the title, with **E**lton, **L**iston, **I**mrie and **A**stor Streets being joined slightly further along by **S**tuart Road, the only one of the sequence not directly next to its predecessor. In between Goodison Road and City Road, a third generation of the family is commemorated. William's son E. Alfred has his name spelt out by **E**spin, **A**skew, **L**inton, **F**rodsham, **R**ipon, **E**mery and **D**yson Streets. This Welsh dynasty had been started in Everton by Owen Elias (1806-80), who built a lot of terraced property on the slopes between Great Homer Street and Netherfield Road North. He named one Elias Street after himself although this is no longer in existence.

Not all streets in Liverpool with Welsh connections were necessarily named by Welsh builders. More recently developed, near the junction of West Derby Road and Belmont Road are **Conwy Drive**, **Gwent Close**, **Cardigan Way** and **Montgomery Way**. These are the results of clearance of terraced streets and the only Welsh influence before this in the area was **Celt Street**, which is now considerably shorter than before due to the recreation ground. There is a newly built **Clwyd Grove** in West Derby, while in the southern end of the city new developments off Riverside Drive have led to the creation of **Moel Famau View**. This is named after the 555 metre high mountain in the Clwydian hills, which can be seen from there on a clear day. In the last couple of years, **Barry Drive**, **Cardiff Way** and **Swansea Close** have all been developed in Garston.

Although not as prominent as the Welsh builders, the Scots did have an influence in the rise of Liverpool. In the city centre, there was a considerable Scottish presence in the Rodney Street area from the beginning of the 19th century. St Andrew's Church was built, as was the Caledonian School and **Caledonia Street** remembers their presence here. Nearby **Melville Place** is named after Viscount Melville, an 18th century politician who was known as 'the uncrowned King of Scotland' due to his passionate speeches in Parliament.

There are some clusters of streets around Edge Lane and Prescot Road that hint at a Scottish influence when they were built. In Fairfield **Balmoral Road**, **Carstairs Road**, **Huntly Road** and **Kelso Road** are all named after Scottish towns. In the nearby Stanley district, **Cheviot Road** and **Grampian Road** are named after mountain ranges, while **Lomond Road** commemorates one of Scotland's highest mountains. **Clyde Road** takes its name from the river that runs through Glasgow and the water theme continues with **Lorne Street**, named after the Firth of Lorne on the west coast. Scottish towns are remembered in Old Swan by **Barrymore Road**, **Dunmore Road**, **Glencairn Road** and **Selkirk Road**. North of the city centre, near to the Costco store, streets named after the Scottish towns of **Greenock Street** and **Paisley Street** have survived but Dundee Street has long gone In Childwall, **Glendevon Road** and **Glenlyon Road** are named after valleys. Nearer to the city centre, off West Derby Road a Scot built **Dunkeld Street** and **Perth Street** in the 1860s.

The biggest group of Scottish themed streets seems to be in Allerton, off Brodie Avenue. Places on the mainland have given names to **Ardmore Road**, **Benmore Road** and **Carrickmore Avenue**, whilst **Arranmore Road**, **Cairnmore Road**, **Glenmore Avenue** and **Lismore Road** are after islands or villages on them. Avonmore Avenue is named after a river, **Lochmore Road** after a loch and **Kirkmore Road** after the Scottish word for church. On the other side of the railway line the Scottish connection continues with **Caithness Road** taking its name from the Highland county of Caithness, **Halkirk Road** from a village in the county and **Stroma Road** an island off the its coast.

To round off, an Isle of Man builder who built a lot of terraced streets in north Liverpool was Richard Costain, who moved to Crosby in 1865. His building company eventually became the Costain Group, which played a part in the construction of the Channel Tunnel. **Costain Street** in Kirkdale is named after him.

LOCAL RELIGIOUS FIGURES AND CHURCHES

I N LIVERPOOL CITY CENTRE there are many reminders of bygone churches and figures associated with them. Citywide, many streets have also been influenced by places of worship, with a number of Church Streets and Church Roads being in existence.

The Metropolitan Cathedral was consecrated in 1967. It would have been completed much earlier and been far bigger, had it not been for the the 2nd World War. Initially there were plans drawn up by Sir Edwin Landseer Lutyens for a building topped by a 510 feet dome but this was never realised despite construction having commenced in 1933. Although his model was replaced by a cheaper version, he has been remembered by a street in Kirkdale, **Lutyens Close**. This is on the same estate as **Scott Close**, named after Sir Giles Gilbert Scott, whose design for the Anglican Cathedral did come to fruition. Scott was only 21 years old when he submitted the designs and the building was still being constructed when he died in 1960. It was eventually completed in 1978, 74 years after building work had begun. These two streets are 1970s additions to the area, **Pugin Street** having been in existence for over a hundred years. This was named after Edward Pugin who had designed a number of churches locally, including Our Lady of Immaculate in St Domingo Road and St Margarets in Anfield, sadly neither building is still standing.

Liverpool's main shopping street, **Church Street** takes its name from St Peters Church, which was built after Liverpool became a parish in its own right in 1699. The church was demolished in 1922 and also gave its name to **Church Alley**, which ran alongside it. An un-named track to the rear of the church was first named Peter Street by 1766. In the late 18th century the name was changed to its current **Peters Lane** when another Peter Street came into existence off Whitechapel. Off Church Street is **Basnett Street**, laid out on land owned by the Basnett family in the mid 18th century. One member of the family, Christopher Basnett, was the first minister of the Key Street Presbyterian Chapel, which stood off Tithebarn Street on the site of the Mercury Court office complex. Another St Peter's Church no longer in existence stood on the corner of Warbreck Moor and **Church Avenue** in Aintree. The foundation stone for this church was laid by the Bishop of Chester in 1876 and it was demolished in the late 1990s, with **Old Church Close** now situated where it once was.

At the rear of St. George's Hall lie St. John's Gardens, which opened in 1904 after the demolition of St. John's Church. The church had been built around 1770 and **St John's Lane** took its name from it, having once been known as Fall Well Lane. The original name had come from the fact it led to the Fall Well, which stood in the vicinity and was Liverpool's main water supply. Another place of worship long demolished is the ancient Chapel of St. Mary Del Key, which in addition to giving its name to one of the original seven streets, Chapel Street, is now commemorated by **Old Churchyard**. This was originally called Chapel Yard in the early 18th century. As land was reclaimed to build Liverpool's docks, the old chapels successor has not been forgotten as **St. Nicholas Place** leads to the landing stage.

The first enclosed garden built in Liverpool was **Wostenholme Square**, developed in the mid 18th century as a select locality on land where the Reverend M. Wostenholme resided. In Chinatown, **Raffles Street** is named after another Reverend, Thomas Stamford Raffles, who in 1811 became minister of Great George Street Congregational Chapel, now the 'Blackie' arts centre.

In the 1850s Holy Cross Church was built in Great Crosshall Street. This was named after St. Patricks Cross, which stood nearby at the junction of Marybone, Tithebarn Street and Vauxhall Road until the late 18th Century. The church was demolished in 2004 to make way for student housing but its pieta statue has been enclosed in a memorial garden in adjacent Standish Street. **Holy Cross Close**, off Addison Street, was developed in the late 20th century. Next to Holy Cross Close is **St. Stephen's Place**, developed at the same time. This is named after an earlier St. Stephen's Street, which had commemorated a church of the same name that stood on Byrom Street. Saint Stephen was the first Christian Martyr, stoned to death around AD36 in Jerusalem. Also in this vicinity is **Marybone**, once part of the ancient Bevington Bush Road. It was named in the late 18th century in reference to the large number of local Irish Catholic immigrants. Marybone is an Anglicisation of Mary Le Bonne, the French term for Virgin Mary meaning 'Mary the Good'. Tucked away off Dale Street, **Quakers**

Alley takes its name from an 18th century Friends Meeting House and burial ground. This stood on the corner with Hackins Hey and had been set up by the Religious Society of Friends, more commonly known as Quakers. They see divine revelation as immediate and individual.

As slum properties began to engulf Old Hall Street in the late 18th century, many merchants moved out towards Everton, around **St. Anne Street**. This was named after St Anne's Church, which was built in 1772 and named after the mother of the Virgin Mary, closing in 1971 and now demolished. Another church built around this time as development took place away from the centre was St. James Church in Toxteth. This was built in 1774 and after closing in 1971 re-opened in 2009 under the care of the Churches Conservation Trust. This has given its name to **St. James Street** and **St. James Place**, the former being part of the old Park Lane with a section of it being re-named after the church was built.

On the corner of Myrtle Street and Hope Street stood the Myrtle Street Baptist Church, which was closed in 1939 and is now a car park. A minister of this in the second half of the 18th century was Hugh Stowell Brown, who gives his name to nearby **Stowell Street**. He administered charity locally and set up a savings bank for his parishioners. Further up Myrtle Street was Holy Innocents Church, which stood on the site of **Minster Court**. This name was arrived at in the early 1990s, having earlier been Myrtle Gardens and Minster Gardens. Near to the corner of Canning Street and Catharine Street is St. Brides Church, named after St Bride (or St. Brigid), one of the three patron saints of Ireland. She was a fifth century nun who founded four monasteries and the church has given its name to **St. Bride Street**.

Canon T. Major Lester (1829-1903) was a vicar in Kirkdale for fifty years, founding the Walton School Board in 1863 and built Major Lester School in 1860. This was financed from begging letters and he also helped to found hospitals. **Major Street** and **Lester Close** in Kirkdale take their names from him. For nearly 80 years, between 1768 and 1847, father and son Henry and Samuel Heathcote were rectors of St. Mary's Church in Walton and **Heathcote Road** remembers them. The church itself has given its name to **St Mary's Avenue**, **Grove**, **Place** and **Lane**. A road close to the church grounds is **Penuel Road**, named after Penuel in Jordan where Jacob saw God.

Although not all of them still stand today, some Catholic churches in the Scotland Road area are remembered by street names. **Silvester Street** took its name from St. Silvesters Church, which was named after St Silvester, Pope from 314-335. On the other side of Scotland Road is St Anthony's Church, which gives its name to **St. Anthony's Place**. This church, still an imposing site today, was built in 1833 to accommodate the expanding population and named after St Anthony, an Egyptian hermit who was the first Christian monk. A former priest of the church was Father Jim O'Reilly, from County Meath in Ireland. In 1970 he expressed concern at the number of people moving out of the area to out of town developments and was a great supporter of the Eldonian scheme that saw local residents re-generate their own community. In the late 1980s he was due to move into a bungalow there in **O'Reilly Court**, named after him, but died before it was completed.

Three new streets have been named since the 1980s. St Joseph's Church stood in Grosvenor Street and is remembered today by **St. Joseph's Crescent**, while another church, St Albans in Denbigh Street gave its name to **St. Albans Court**. **St Gerards Close** stands near the site of St Gerards Church. Within the close is the statue of St Gerard that had belonged to the school of the same name prior to its closure and re-opening as the North Liverpool Community Justice Centre in 2005. As the court is non-denominational the statue could not stay there.

In West Derby, the Christopher Grange Blind Institute was opened in 1972. This was founded as long ago as 1841 as the Catholic Blind Asylum in Islington then renamed after secretary Christopher Taylor when it moved into these premises. The original founder, The Very Reverend Doctor Thomas Youens is remembered by **Youens Way**, which connects the institute to East Prescot Road. Youens was rector of the catholic St Nicholas pro cathedral in Copperas Hill and noted in Liverpool for his work with poor people, especially his vast interest in the blind.

St. Oswald's Catholic Church in Old Swan was founded in 1842 and gives its name to **St. Oswald's Street**, which was once part of Edge Lane. Off this is **Maddocks Street**, which is named after Canon Maddocks, the first priest in the church. This was the first street in Liverpool to be named after a local Catholic churchman and remained the only one until **Whiteside Close** was developed over 100 years later. This remembered Thomas Whiteside, who in 1911 became Liverpool's first Archbishop. Also in the Old Swan/Stoneycroft area stand three Russian named streets. They were named after evangelist Heber Radcliffe, who owned land locally and went on a mission to Russia. As a surprise for him on his return, the long roads of **Kremlin Drive**, **Moscow Drive** and **Russian Drive** were laid out, with the latter two being linked by the smaller **Russian Avenue**. Nearby, **Brookland Road East** and **Brookland Road West** are named after a former rector of Liverpool, Archdeacon Brooks, who owned the land on which it was built. It had been acquired by his ancestor Joseph Brooks in 1782.

In Wavertree, **Church Road** and **Church Road North** were created by the Wavertree Enclosure Act of 1768, allowing for the division of land into fields. The initially unnamed lanes were later named after Holy Trinity Church, which dates from 1794. Staying in Wavertree, St. Mary's Church in Victoria Park was built in 1837 and replaced a Wesleyan Methodist Chapel that is now remembered by **Wesley Place**.

Near to Otterspool, a Puritan settlement developed in the 17th century known as 'Little Jordan'. This was sited next to the River Jordan, which is now mainly diverted underground. Jericho Farm was set up and this was connected to Aigburth Road (then Park Lane) by an un-named lane that became **Jericho Lane**. The farmhouse was demolished in 1960 but **Jericho Farm Close** was developed and named after the settlement. Monks from Stanlawe Abbey in Cheshire once owned land in Garston. Some streets in this area are named in relation to this, including **Priory Street**, which takes its name from a religious house that monks live in. **Monkfield Way** is named after an area known as the Monks Field, situated where the railway line forks to go down to the docks.

In Woolton, there is a **James Road** and **James Court**. These are named after the St. James Wesleyan Methodist and United Reform church at the bottom of **Church Road South**, which along with **Church Road** is named after the Church of St. Peters, completed in 1826. **St. Mary's Street** in Woolton takes its name from St. Mary's Church, which was built in 1860 due to the growing influx of Irish Catholics in the vicinity as St. Benet's Priory in Watergate Lane was by then inadequate. St Benets itself is remembered by **Priors Close**, **Priory Way** and **Priorsfield Road**. The religious theme continues off Out Lane, with **Monks Way**, **Bishops Court** and **Deacon Court** being named after church positions, and **Abbey Court** completing the group.

St. Stephen's Church in Belle Vale has been responsible for the naming of **Churchfield Road**, **St Stephens Close** and **Vicarage Lawn**. According to the New Testament, St Stephen was the first Christian martyr, being stoned to death in AD34. In Chidlwall, **St Paschal Baylon Boulevard** leads to St Paschal Baylon Church, which closed in 2011, a sign of the times as the Catholic Church struggled with increasing costs and a fall in congregation sizes.

When the Eldonian Village was built in the 1980s, Liverpool's two leading churchmen at the time were commemorated due to the support they had given to the project. **Archbishop Worlock Court** is named after the Roman Catholic Archbishop of Liverpool, Derek Worlock, who died in 1996 after serving the city for twenty years. The Anglican bishop, the Right Reverend David Sheppard was remembered by **Bishop Sheppard Court**. Sheppard, who held the position for 22 years, had earlier played cricket for 15 years for Sussex, as well as captaining England for a short time. After retiring in 1997 he was made a life peer and sat on the Labour benches in the House of Lords, dying of cancer in 2005. The two jointly published a book, *Better Together*, the title of which was borrowed from the Eldonians motto: 'We Do It Better Together'.

In the 1990s, development took place on land fronting the Anglican Cathedral, with **Dean Dillistone Court** and **Dean Patey Court** both remembering former deans. Dillistone was dean from 1956 to 1963 before Patey took over the role for the next twenty years, overseeing the cathedral's completion and visit from Pope John Paul II. To mark the new millennium an environmentally friendly development was built at the back of the Church of the Good Shepherd in Croxteth. **Good Shepherd Close** was developed by Riverside Housing in 1999 and contains solar panels and low flush lavatories, amongst other things.

WIDER RELIGIOUS INFLUENCES

THROUGHOUT LIVERPOOL there are a number of streets named after biblical characters, religious figures or cathedrals. Most of these streets were developed during the 19ᵗʰ and early 20ᵗʰ centuries, although some have only been named in the past decade or so.

Perhaps the most well known of Liverpool's religious streets are in an area known as the Holyland in Toxteth. This is situated between Beresford Road, Mill Street, Park Road and Park Hill Road and its nickname comes from the biblical names given to the streets. **Moses Street** is named after the Hebrew prophet who was founder of the Jewish people, while **David Street** commemorates the King of Judea and Israel who founded Jerusalem as the nation's capital. **Isaac Street** is named after Isaac, father of Jacob, whose twelve sons became the patriarchs of the twelve tribes of Israel, while Jacob himself is remembered in **Jacob Street**. Running across all four streets is **Grace Street**, which in Christian theology is a term meaning unearned favour bestowed on people by God.

Off Northumberland Street in Toxteth is **Doddridge Street**, which is named after Philip Doddridge (1702-51), a non-conformist hymn writer who wrote *The Rise and Progress Of Religion in the Soul*. At the end of Doddridge Road is **Tillotson Close**, named after a 17th century Archbishop of Canterbury, John Tillotson. In the Granby area of Toxteth, **Kinglsey Road** is named after Charles Kingsley, an Anglican priest who was known for his liberal views and supported Darwin's theory of evolution. He also taught history at Cambridge in the 1860s and his novels displayed sympathy with the economically depressed classes of his day. Off Kingsley Road is **Eversley Road**, after the Hampshire town where he was a rector from 1844 to 1860. A standalone street in Aigburth is **Hadassah Grove**, developed off Lark Lane in the 1840s. Hadassah is the Hebrew name of the heroine Esther, the Jewish Queen of Persia who managed to save her people from annihilation at the hands of Prince Haman.

In between Scotland Road and Vauxhall Road, a leading figure of the English Reformation, Thomas Cranmer (1489-1556) is remembered in **Cranmer Street**. As Archbishop of Canterbury under Henry VIII, he oversaw the removal of the Pope's name from every prayer book and proclaimed the King the Head of the English Church. However, when Henry's daughter Mary, a Catholic, came to the throne in 1553 Cranmer was arrested for treason and burnt at the stake on 21st March 1556. Someone else who suffered the same fate at the hands of 'Bloody Mary' was Hugh Latimer, after whom **Latimer Street** is named. He was the Bishop of Worcester and burnt on 16th October 1555, one of 300 to be condemned for heresy during her reign. These two streets run off **Athol Street**, which takes its name from John Murray, 1st Duke of Athol (1660-1724). He was the grandson of the 7th Earl of Derby and fought in the Glorious Revolution of 1688 that saw the overthrow of the Catholic King James II. Nearby John Bird Sumner, Archbishop of Canterbury from 1848 to 1862 and a former Bishop of Chester, has given his name to **Sumner Close**, which stands on the site of an earlier Sumner Street. It was an ironic twist of fate that when all these streets were built, it was Irish Catholic immigrants that tended to inhabit them. In the early 20th century a local councillor tried in vain to have the names changed, even climbing up walls to try and take the signs down.

Three medieval churchmen are remembered in Kirkdale. **Becket Street** is named after Thomas a Becket (c1118-70), the Archbishop of Canterbury who was murdered by four of the King's men, although not on the King's orders. William of Wykeham (1324-1404) gives his name to **Wykeham Street**. He was Bishop of Winchester and father of the English public schools system. **Wulstan Street** honours St Wulstan who was the last surviving English bishop after the Norman Conquest of 1066, remaining as Bishop of Worcester until 1095, twenty years longer than any other English bishop managed to survive for. Sandwiched between these streets is **Newman Street**, named after John Henry Newman (1801-90), an outstanding religious thinker and essayist who became a cardinal after his conversion to the Catholic Church.

Also in Kirkdale, **Westminster Road** was widened in the 1860s and re-named from Field lane. It is named after Westminster Abbey in London, where English monarchs are crowned and many are buried along with a number of other prominent citizens. Westminster Road leads on to **Lambeth Road**, named after Lambeth Abbey in London, the Archbishop of Canterbury's principal residence. It has another junction with **Melrose Road,** after Melrose Abbey in Scotland, dating from the 12th century although much of it is now in ruins. Other streets in this area to be named after abbeys are **Easby Road, Fonthill Street**, **Fonthill Close** and **Furness Street**. Fonthill Abbey was in Wiltshire and has been demolished for nearly 200 years, while Furness Abbey and Easby Abbey in Cumbria and North Yorkshire respectively are now in ruins. Fountains Abbey, near Ripon in Yorkshire is probably Britain's most known monastic ruin and is remembered by **Fountains Road** and **Fountains Close**.

In Everton, two long disappeared streets off Netherfield Road have re-surfaced since the millennium. **Joshua Close** is named after Joshua, who succeeded Moses as leader of the Israelites after his death while **Calmet Close** commemorates Benedictine monk Augustine Calmet, (1672-1757), who provided explanations of the Bible. Also in Everton, **Spurgeon Close** has replaced an earlier Spurgeon Street. This is named after Charles Haddon Spurgeon (1834-92), a preacher who founded Spurgeons College in London for the training of men in Christian service.

In Orrell Park, **Grace Road** is named after the Grace Church in New York City, which was built in a restrained Gothic Revival style between 1846 and 1849. **Renwick Road** remembers American architect James Renwick, who built the church as his first major project. He went on to design the Smithsonian Institute in Washington DC and St Patrick's Cathedral in New York. In Kirkdale, another architect is remembered by **Teulon Close**. Samuel Teulon designed over fifty churches in southern England and the Midlands in the Victorian period.

Off Townsend Lane in Cabbage Hall a number of streets are named after religious buildings and church positions. **Abbey Road** and **Monastery Road** take their names from communities of monks, **Cathedral Road** from the principal church of a diocese and **Chapel Road** from a place of worship within a church. **Bishop Road** is named after the clergyman in charge of a whole diocese, while **Curate Road** and **Vicar Road** are named after types of local clergymen. **Rector Road** comes from the figure that is the head priest of a religious institution. **Canon Road** could be named either after a member of a cathedral or a church decree. Slightly further down Townsend Lane, **Wycliffe Road** is named after John Wycliffe (1330-84), a philosopher who was a forerunner of the Reformation, believing Christians should have a direct relationship with God without the need for parish priests.

In the first decade of the 20th century, Charles Berrington of Bedford acquired the Heathfield Park Estate in Wavertree and set about development. He named **Charles Berrington Road** after himself, the full name rather than just the surname being used so as to avoid confusion with Barrington Road. His cousin and foreman joiner was named Litchefield and this was corrupted to form **Lichfield Road**. Lichfield is a cathedral city and all the other streets on the estate, between Charles Berrington Road and Church Road are named after cathedrals. Amongst these is **Truro Road**, after the first cathedral to be consecrated since the Reformation and **Hereford Road**, after Hereford Cathedral, which has on exhibit a 1290 map of the world portraying Jerusalem as the centre. Other cathedral cities are commemorated in **Beverley Road**, **Bristol Road**, **Coventry Road**, **Newcastle Road**, **Norwich Road** and **Peterborough Road**.

Cathedral cities are also commemorated by a number of streets in Garston, near to Banks Road. **Lincoln Street** is named after a cathedral on which building commenced in the 11th century, while Durham Cathedral, which was finished in 1133, gives its name to **Durham Street**. Canterbury Cathedral, which was started in the 12th century after an earlier church was destroyed by fire, is remembered by **Canterbury Street** and **York Street** and **York Way** takes their names from York Minster, a cathedral that retains more medieval glass than any other.

Off Bentham Drive and Bowland Avenue in Childwall some saints are commemorated. A 3rd century saint and martyr, St. Alban, was a Roman soldier who converted to Christianity and was be-headed for sheltering a priest. The site of the town where this occurred, Verulanium was later named St. Albans after him, as was **Alban Road**. In the 4th century St. Basil wrote Christian doctrines that are still followed by most Orthodox monks today and **Basil Close** and **Basil Road** remember him. The patron saint of travellers, St. Christopher, of whom there is no documentary evidence of his existence, gives his name to **Christopher Close** and **Christopher Way**. **Dominic Close**, **Dominic Road** and **Francis Way** remember two founders of Christian orders. St. Dominic was a Spanish theologian who founded the Dominicans, known as the Black Friars in this country, while St. Francis of Assisi was founder of the Franciscan Monks. **Gregory Close** and **Gregory Way** are named after St. Gregory, Pope 590-604, known as the 'father of Christian worship'.

In addition to the saints in Childwall, two scholars also have streets named after them. **Lanfranc Way** and **Lanfranc Close** are named after Lanfranc, 11th century Italian ecclesiastic who was Archbishop of Canterbury from 1070 to 1089 after being installed by William the Conqueror. Origen, who gives his name to **Origen Road,** was an Egyptian writer and theologian who taught in Palestine, was imprisoned for a year in AD 250 and died three years later, weakened by injuries sustained there. Over the other side of the old railway line, now part of the Liverpool loop line cycle path, there is **Walsingham Road**, from the Shrine of Our Lady of Walsingham in Norfolk, where the Virgin Mary is said to have appeared to a local noblewoman in 1061.

Nearly all of the streets with religious connections mentioned so far were developed before the 2nd World War, but more recently there have been streets with this theme built in Croxteth Park. **Lindisfarne Drive** remembers the Celtic monastery of Lindisfarne. This was founded in 653 and one of its early priors St. Cuthbert gives his name to **St. Cuthberts Close**. The west Hebridean monastery of Iona, established in the 6th century is commemorated in **Iona Close**, while **Tewkesbury Close** takes its name from an 11th century abbey in Gloucestershire.

LITERARY LIVERPOOL

THROUGHOUT LIVERPOOL there are clusters of streets named after famous literary characters. Some famous writers are named more than once, while others are not featured at all. Some less well-known writers are present too. In many ways, it has all come down to the personal tastes of the developer, with the most recent builders still using literary figures when naming streets.

Joshua Rose, who owned a lot of land in the Scotland Road and Great Homer Street area at the turn of the 19th century, was the first developer to build streets in Liverpool with a literary theme. He named **Rose Hill**, **Rose Place** and **Rose Vale** after himself, but in the other streets his interest in the arts, especially poetry, was evident. There was a road known as Sickmans Lane as it was where victims of the Bubonic Plague had been interred and buried in the 14th century. Rose then formally named this **Addison Street**, after Joseph Addison (1672-1719), a poet who regularly contributed to *The Tatler* and *The Spectator*. On the other side of Byrom Street streets were named after poets of an even earlier age. **Chaucer Street** was named after Geoffrey Chaucer, author of the 14th century *Canterbury Tales* and **Juvenal Street** commemorates a Roman satirical poet, Decimus Junius Juvenalis (65-128 AD). He painted a vivid description of Roman society with his satires. **Comus Street** is not written after a poet or author, but a play itself. *Comus,* a masque (something that involves singing, dancing and acting), was written by John Milton and first presented in Ludlow in 1634, but developed further in the early 1800s. **Talieson Street** remembers a Welsh poet from the 6th century, some of whose poems are published in the Book of Talieson, which was compiled some 700 years later.

By 1810, Rose had laid out **Great Homer Street** as a continuation of Fox Street, but it was not for another ten years that it was built upon and twenty before it extended further than Rose Vale. Homer was a Greek poet from c.850 BC who composed two epic poems in an impersonal style detailing events that happened many years before they were written. One of these poems, *The Iliad*, is remembered by **Iliad Street**. This poem dealt with events of the Trojan War, fought between the Greeks and the city of Troy in Turkey. Linking Great Homer Street with Iliad Street is **Sheridan Street**, named after Richard Brinsley Sheridan (1751-1816), a dramatist who managed the Drury Lane theatre in London and also served in Parliament as under-secretary for foreign affairs and secretary to the treasury. Soon after Great Homer Street, **Roscommon Street** was laid out by Rose and named after Wentworth Dillon, 4th Earl of Roscommon (1633-85). He formed a literary society with John Dryden (1631-1700), after whom **Dryden Street** is named. Dryden wrote many poems depicting historical figures, such as *Heroic Stanzas*, which commemorated Oliver Cromwell.

At the Kirkdale Road end of Great Homer Street is **Medea Street**, named after the Greek tragedy play *Medea*. The hero of this play, Jason, is commemorated by **Jason Street** and **Jason Walk,** which runs off it. These streets have only been developed since the Second World War, continuing the theme of a number of Greek (although not literary) named streets that have disappeared such as Candia Street and Crete Street, which have survived by way of tower blocks. Two streets that disappeared were Patmos and Zante Street. These names were wiped off the Liverpool street maps for many years, but have now returned again since the millennium in the form of **Patmos Close** and **Zante Close**, named after islands, the latter of which is now a popular holiday destination. **Mitylene Street**, named after another Greek island, still exists in a much shortened form off Netherfield Road North. In another part of Everton off West Derby Road it is worth pointing out a standalone Greek Street, **Hygeia Street**, named after the Greek goddess of medicine and from which the word hygiene derives. It is somewhat ironic though that this street adjoins the old Ogdens tobacco factory.

Going back to literature Sir Walter Scott (1771-1832) was a Scottish poet and novelist whose historical works created a great interest in Scottish traditions. His works are remembered especially in Aigburth, with **Marmion Road** being named after an 1808 poem of the same name and **Ivanhoe Road**, **Mannering Road** and **Waverley Road** being named after novels (*Ivanhoe, Guy Mannering* and *Waverley*). The principal character in *Guy Mannering* is Harry Bertram, commemorated in **Bertram Road**. Another character from one of Scott's poems is Lochinvar, who features in *Marmion*. He gives his name to **Lochinvar Street** in Walton, which is situated next to **Peveril**

Street, named after Scott's novel *Peveril Peak*. In Everton, between St Anne Street and Shaw Street **Roderick Street**, **Rokeby Street** and **Rokeby Close** remember two more of Scott's poems. Elsewhere in Everton off Netherfield Road North, **Robsart Street** is named after Amy Robsart, a character from Scott's novel *Kenilworth*. This street was once named Tarleton Street, after the family of merchants who had a house there, but it was changed after Everton's absorption into Liverpool to avoid confusion. **Abbotsford Road** in Norris Green remembers the last home of Scott, Abbotsford House, on the banks of the Tweed in Melrose. In the south of the city, **Lammermoor Road** in Mossley Hill is named after his novel *The Bride of Lammermoor*, set in the early 18th century.

One of the reasons that Sir Walter Scott turned to novel writing from poetry was due to the popularity of Lord Byron (1788-1824), one of the most versatile of the romantic poets. He is remembered by **Byron Street**, off Banks Road in Garston, which is next to **Otway Street**, named after dramatist Thomas Otway (1652-85) and **Shakespeare Street**, named after the world's most famous playwright William Shakespeare (1564-1616). Another street in this vicinity is **Marlowe Close**, which was inspired by Christopher Marlowe, who was stabbed to death in a tavern brawl in Deptford in 1593, aged 29. His play *Edward II* was a model for Shakespeare's *Richard II* and *Richard III*. Also present is **Shelley Grove**, named after another romantic poet, Percy Bysshe Shelley (1792-1822).

For such a revered playwright, William Shakespeare is not as widely remembered in Liverpool as might be expected. In addition to being commemorated in Garston, there is a **Shakespeare Close** in Everton while **Verona Street** in Anfield commemorates one of his plays, *The Two Gentlemen of Verona*. The only cluster of streets is in the Bank Hall area. **Celia Street** and **Rosalind Way** are named after characters from *As you Like It*, while a character named Beatrice appears in both this play and *Twelfth Night* and gives her name to **Beatrice Street**. *Henry V* characters gave their names to **Falstaff Street** and **Hotspur Street** with **Oberon Street**, **Miranda Place** and **Portia Street** being named after characters from *A Midsummer Nights Dream*, *The Tempest* and *The Merchant of Venice* respectively. **Hector Place** is named after a character from *Troilus and Cressida*, while **Macbeth Street** and **Othello Close** remember titles of Shakespeare's plays. There are more Shakespeare themed streets over the Liverpool/Sefton boundary in Bootle.

In Toxteth, between North Hill Street and Upper Warwick Street, the work of Charles Dickens (1812-70), whose novels provided an acute social commentary of the time have been well remembered. Several of these original streets have been demolished and rebuilt as closes. Amongst those present are **Barkis Close** and **Micawber Close**, named after characters in Dickens's novel *David Copperfield*. There is also a **Copperfield Close** itself and the novels of *Little Dorrit*, *Dombey and Son* and *Nicholas Nickleby* are all remembered by **Dorrit Street**, **Dombey Street**, and **Nickleby Close**. These are in addition to a **Dickens Street**, which needs no explanation, as well as **Pecksniff Street**, named after a character from *Martin Chuzzlewitt*. One of Dickens first works was the *Pickwick Papers*, published in monthly instalments between 1836 and 1837. **Tupman Street**, **Weller Street** and **Winkle Street** are named after characters from this, while the novel itself is remembered by **Pickwick Street**.

As well as being well represented in Toxteth, Dickens has another cluster of streets named after his novels on an estate between Earle Road and Tunnel Road in Edge Hill. This was re-developed in the early 1980s, with the new closes retaining the names of the old terraced streets that disappeared. Noah Claypole, a character from *Oliver Twist* gives his name to **Claypole Close**, while **Barnet Close** takes its name from the Barnet Union Workhouse, where it is said a friend of Charles Dickens visited and heard a boy ask for more, an inspiration for part of the novel. Characters from the novel *Our Mutual Friend* influence the other Dickens streets. These are **Lightwood Drive** (Mortimer Lightwood), **Rokesmith Avenue** (John Rokesmith), **Wilfer Close** (Bella Wilfer) and **Wrayburn Close** (Eugene Wrayburn). **Acton Way** has connections with Dickens' novel *Bleak House*. The village in Suffolk was the home of William Jennens, known as the Acton Miser who died leaving an estate worth £2 million but having outlived all his executors and beneficiaries. The legal wrangles over the estate were the basis for the Jarndyce and Jarndyce case which was central to the *Bleak House* plot. The novel's theme is maintained with **Hawdon Court**, named after one of its characters Captain Hawdon

Near to these Dickens streets, some American poets of the Victorian era have been honoured off Smithdown Road. Oliver Wendell Holmes (1809-94), a writer of witty verse is remembered by **Wendell Street** and **Holmes Street**, while John Greenleaf Whittier (1807-92) gives his name to **Greenleaf Street** and **Whittier Street**. **Cullen Street** commemorates William Cullen Bryant (1794-1878). **Longfellow Street**, which runs across the top of all five of these streets, is named after Henry Wadsworth Longfellow (1807-82), the first American to have a bust made in his honour in poets' corner in Westminster Abbey. A less well-known American poet, Henry Vandyke (1852-1933) is remembered by **Vandyke Street**. Parallel to Longfellow Street, the theme turns to British writers with **Boswell Street** being named after James Boswell (1740-95), a friend and biographer to poet Samuel Johnson. **Wordsworth Street** commemorates William Wordsworth (1770-1850), one of the most influential of the Romantic poets. Finally, **Newstead Road** is named not after a poet but after one of their homes. Newstead Abbey in Nottinghamshire was the ancestral home of Lord Byron, who as mentioned earlier has a street named after him in Garston.

Herman Melville, best remembered for *Moby Dick*, wrote the semi-autobiographical novel *Redburn* in 1849, which describes his experiences in Liverpool as a cabin boy. Melville Street in Toxteth is not actually named after him but when surrounding streets were demolished the opportunity was taken to name a new street off it **Redburn Close**.

One of the great Victorian poets was Lord Alfred Tennyson (1809-92). He was the first poet to be made a peer of the realm and had produced several blank verse plays and an epic by the age of fifteen. In 1842 he published the two volume *Poems*, which included *Morte d'Arthur*, an idyll based on the Arthurian legend, which is a group of tales from the Middle Ages, which spanned from the 5th to 15th centuries, about the legendary Arthur, King of the Britons. His second Arthurian work, *Idylls of the King*, was written between 1859 and 1885 and these tales are remembered between North Hill Street and Upper Warwick Street in Toxteth. **Merlin Street** is named after a counsellor of King Arthur and **Modred Street** after his nephew, with **Elaine Street, Enid Street, Geraint Street** and **Gwendoline Street** also being named after people from the legend. **Celtic Street** takes its name from the Celtic origins of the Arthurian legend, while **Maud Street** is named after one of Tennyson's other works, *Maud and Other Poems*. Tennyson himself was commemorated by Tennyson Street and later Tennyson Walk, although this has been lost to redevelopment in recent years.

Thackeray Close, **Thackeray Place** and **Thackeray Street** in Toxteth were named after William Makepeace Thackeray, who was the author of *Vanity Fair* and *Henry Esmond*. He was a writer of the realistic novel, emphasising social systems and was a rival to Charles Dickens. Near to the junction of Breck Road and Belmont Road in Anfield there are three streets named after his novels, **Esmond Street** (*Henry Esmond*), **Pendennis Street** (*Pendennis)* and **Newcombe Street** (*The Newcombes*). There is also a **Becky Street**, named after Becky Sharp, a character from *Vanity Fair* and **Castlewood Road**, after Frank and Rachel Castlewood, the two main characters in Henry Esmond. Alongside this group of streets is **Sedley Street**, which although not linked to Thackeray, does have literary connections. Sir Charles Sedley (1639-1701) was an English dramatist and poet whose comedy plays include *Bellamira* and *The Mulberry Garden*.

Benjamin Disraeli, who was Prime Minister in 1868 and 1874-80, also pursued a writing career. He has five streets in Anfield named after his novels; **Lothair Road**, **Alroy Road**, **Sybil Road**, **Coningsby Road** and **Tancred Road**.

The development of Edge Hill had gathered pace by the 1860s as merchants villas became swamped by terraced housing, with some of the main streets of the old settlement being re-named. Lord Street was divided into two and named **Overbury Street**, after poet Sir Thomas Overbury (1581-1613) and **Overton Street**, after Richard Overton, leader of the Leveller movement, a 17th century political group, who wrote *Mans Morality* in 1643. King Street was re-named **Kinglake Street**, after Alexander William Kinglake (1809-91, who in 1844 wrote *Eothen: or Traces of Travel Brought home From the East*. This was an account of travels ten years earlier and he also wrote a history of the Crimean War. Other Edge Hill Streets named after literary figures are **Shenstone Street** and **Sidney Place**. The former was named after poet and essayist William Shenstone (1714-63), writer of *The Schoolmistress* and *The Judgement of Hercules,* while the latter takes its name from Sir Philip Sidney (1554-86). He was a courtier to Queen Elizabeth I and his poetry was published posthumously following his premature death from a musket wound suffered during a skirmish with some Spanish soldiers.

In the late 1990s new development occurred on the site of a former school off Childwall Valley Road and Chelwood Avenue. This has led to some 20th century literary figures being remembered. **Baldwin Avenue** is named after Stanley Baldwin, who was Prime Minister from 1923-4 and 1935-7. He later became a writer and his books include *Classics* and the *Plain Man and Peace and Goodwill*. John Masefield, who was poet laureate 1930-67, spent his sea cadetship on Merseyside and the anchor of his training ship, HMS Conway stands outside the Merseyside Maritime Museum entrance. He published a book of poems, *Sea Water Ballads* in 1902. He has written more poems commemorating events on Merseyside than any other poet and is remembered by **Masefield Grove**. Another poet laureate, from 1972-84, was John Betjeman who also wrote a number of books about architecture. He gives his name to **Betjeman Grove** while **Swinburne Close** is named after Algernon Charles Swinburne (1837-1909), whose *Poems and Ballads* in 1866 caused a famous Victorian literary scandal due to its sexual content.

In Walton next to Walton Park cemetery, a very recent development is **Noonan Close**, named after Robert Noonan, who wrote *The Ragged Trousered Philanthropists*, under the penname Robert Tressel. Noonan lived in Sussex but was emigrating to Canada in 1911 when he took ill in Liverpool and died in the Royal Infirmary. He was buried in a pauper's grave in Walton Cemetery and his book was published posthumously, with the grave's location now marked with a fitting gravestone. The close is a nice addition to **Tressell Street**, which is situated in another part of Walton off Breeze Lane

SPEKE AND OTHER LOCAL
AUTHORITY DEVELOPMENTS

I N THE INTER WAR YEARS large scale development by Liverpool corporation took place in outlying districts of the city in order to house people from the slums of the inner-city.

Generally speaking, most of the streets were named after towns, which gave a virtually unending supply of names to choose from. However, there were some exceptions, most notably in Speke, while the Militant Tendency had some novel names for streets when they built new houses in the 1980s.

For centuries Speke was no more than a scattered group of cottages and a collection of farms that were inter-linked by lanes. It had a population of no more than 400, but this changed in 1921 following the death of Adelaide Watt, the last owner of Speke Hall. The house itself was taken over by the National Trust, but the majority of the estate was bought by Liverpool Corporation and earmarked for a development to house people being moved from the inner city. The aim was to build a satellite town that would be a countrywide model, ending social segregation by providing accommodation and amenities side by side for all sections of the community. Some of the old lanes remained, with a lot of new roads being named after local landmarks and woodland.

The most famous owners of Speke Hall had been the Norris family, who were lords of the manor for nearly 400 years until the mid 18th century. Surprisingly, no streets are named directly after them, but an estate that belonged to them at Blackrod, near Bolton, gives its name to **Blackrod Avenue**. One of the earlier lords of the manor, Benedict de Gerneth is commemorated in **Gerneth Road** and **Gerneth Close**. He had taken over the land not long after the Domesday survey of 1086 and one of his descendants, Roger Gerneth was Speke's chief forester, appointed by the King to administer forest law, in the 12th century. In ancient times challenge fights used to take place between the villages of Hale, Halewood and Speke. These took place on a piece of land at the boundary of all three, named the Conleach, which gives its name to **Conleach Road**.

Speke Town Lane is one of the original lanes of the estate, although it is now considerably shorter than it was. This led to Speke Town Farm, which stood near the junction of Speke Boulevard and Speke Hall Road. Another lane to be shortened was **Woodend Lane**, which led to Woodend Farm, presumably named as it was at the end of a wood. Some of the first corporation houses to be built were on **Hale Road**, which already existed leading to the village of Hale. All Saints Church, which had been built in 1876 gave its name to **All Saints Road** and **Speke Church Road**, the latter of which was part of a longer lane called Hall Lane that led all the way to Speke Hall. **School Way** takes its name from the original sandstone village school, which was replaced by the much larger Stockton Wood Comprehensive in 1940. Built around the time of the church, the old school building is still in use today as the church hall.

An obvious example of a farm that had to make way for the estate and been remembered in street names is **Goldfinch Farm Road**, while **Sutton Wood Road** remembers its owners. Also there is **Greyhound Farm Road**, which was also the local pub until Adelaide Watt took its licence away. Its last owner, Thomas Critchley, is remembered by **Critchley Road** and off this is **Harland Green**, named after George Harland, the last occupant of Home Farm Cottage which is now the café in Speke Hall. Other farms remembered are **Blacklock Hall Road**, **Tewit Hall Road** and **Tewit Hall Close**.

A farm still in existence is Linner Farm, on Halebank Road. This gave its name to **Linner Road** and probably derives from the 14th century park of Linnall in Hale. Ramsbrook Farm is also in existence in Halebank, taking its name from the Rams Brook, a stream that once flowed right through the present day estate. In addition to the farm, the stream has also given its name to **Ramsbrook Road** and **Ramsbrook Close**. Another farm between Speke and Hale is Heath Gate Farm, after which **Heathgate Avenue** is named.

Speke Hall is very well known locally, but a smaller hall that is remembered is Lovel's Hall, after which **Lovel Road** and **Lovel Way** are named. This was situated close to the junction of the M57 link road and Speke-Widnes road and was named by John Lovel who acquired it through marriage in the late 14th century. The builders of the hall were the Holland family, who are commemorated by **Holland Road**, off Damwood Road. The hall came into the hands of the Earls of

Derby after the 15th century Wars of the Roses and although long since disappeared, its outline and filled in moat can still be seen from the air.

As well as local farms and buildings being commemorated, a number of woodland areas also have streets in Speke named after them, many of which are still in existence. **Damwood Road** and **East Damwood Road** take their name from the Dam Wood, which was situated on the site of the airport runway and also gave rise to a farm of the same name. Stockton's Wood and The Clough are two remaining pieces of woodland in the grounds of Speke Hall and they give their names to **Clough Road** and **Stockton Wood Road**. The timbers used to build Speke Hall are said to have come from The Clough. Even nearer to the built up area of Speke is Little Heath Wood, on the corner of Dungeon Lane and Hale Road. **Little Heath Road** is named after this.

Over the county boundary in the Cheshire borough of Halton are Mill Wood and the Clamley Park plantation. These give their names to **Millwood Road**, **East Millwood Road** and **Clamley Road**. Further afield, on the northern fringe of Hough Green is the Alder Wood, from which **Alderwood Avenue** is named. Harefield, a piece of land that gives its name to **Harefield Road** and **Harefield Green**, lies off Lower Road. Presumably this name simply comes from a field that hares inhabited. **Leveret Road**, off East Millwood Road, takes its name from the leveret, which is a small hare.

Although local history influenced many of the street names in Speke, as time went on the newer streets were named less imaginatively. Main roads east of Western Avenue were laid out on a grid pattern, with **Western Avenue** forming the gateway to the estate from Speke Boulevard and **Central Way** and **Central Avenue** leading away in opposite directions from the shopping area. Old Hutte Lane was re-named **Eastern Avenue** and the western/eastern theme continued with the relatively minor **Northern Road** and **Southern Road**. The roads circling the pedestrian precinct were mundanely named **North Parade** and **South Parade**.

Many of the greens and closes in Speke, which were built off the main roads, were named after towns and villages. **Ardwick Road**, **Burnage Close**, **Heaton Close** and **Withington Road** were all named after district of Manchester, while Wirral places have given their names to **Prenton Green**, **Upton Close** and **Upton Green**. The last part of the estate to be built was the Dymchurch in the 1960s and 70s, something of a planning disaster which gave rise to many social problems. It has since been re-modelled and is known as Phoenix Park. Original streets that survive with a Home Counties theme are **Dymchurch Road**, **Lenham Way**, **Bexhill Close** and **Bognor Close**.

Work on the Norris Green estate started in 1926 and a large number of the streets are named after places in Cumbria. Examples include **Scargreen Avenue** and **Stainburn Avenue**, which are named after places, and **Dunnerdale Road** and **Branstree Avenue**, which take their names from fells. In Dovecot, where building started in 1930, places from different corners of the country are remembered. **Ancroft Road**, **Colwell Road**, **Croxdale Road** and **Gainford Road** take their names from northeast towns and villages, while **Broadoak Road**, **Chedworth Road**, **Somerford Road** and **Winstone Road** are named after places in Gloucestershire. **Grovehurst Avenue**, **Kemsley Road**, **Lunsford Road** and **Lynsted Road** represent Kent place names. In Gillmoss, more than 25 streets were named after places in Devon and Cornwall, including **Falmouth Road**, **Tintagel Road** and **Petherick Road**. In nearby Walton some more imagination has been used with two streets. **Caspian Road** is named after the Caspian Sea in Asia and **Java Road** from one of the islands that make up the country of Indonesia.

In Netherley, which was mainly built in the 1960s and has been largely re-developed since, **Naylorsfield Drive** and **Naylor's Road** are named after former landowners in the area. In terms of place names Wiltshire is a common theme here, with **Deptford Close**, **Durrington Brook** and **Stapleford Road,** as well as Cumbria with **Honister Close**, **Kirkbride Close** and **Ulverston Close** amongst others. However like Speke the farming connections, local buildings and families have been well remembered. **Crabtree Close** is named after Crabtree House, which was demolished to make way for the section of Caldway Drive between Wood Lane and Netherley Road. George Tuffin, who ran a market garden there in the early 20th century, gives his name to **Tuffins Corner**. Very near to Crabtree Lodge was Garden Lodge, the home in 1841 of shipping entrepreneur John Bibby, which gives rise to **Garden Lodge Grove** today. **Holt Lane**, which is named after Holt Hall farm, runs to an adult training centre and then becomes a pedestrian track leading to the clubhouse of Childwall golf course. **Yeoman Fold** comes from the term for a man who owns and farms a small estate and **Glebe Hey** from a piece of land that yields revenue.

Farms have not been forgotten when the area of Childwall at the bottom of Childwall Valley Road was developed either, with **Cockshead Road** being named after a farm that stood in an area and **Capstick Crescent** after its owners.

Streets named after place names are repeated in other corporation developments around the city, but during the 1980s some different names were used. The Left Wing City Council, led by John Hamilton and Derek Hatton embarked on a major house-building programme under the Urban Re-generation Strategy. The slum clearance saw a lot of street names disappear altogether and several more re-named as closes or ways. In addition to this, a number of whole new names were introduced reflecting the Council's Socialist tendencies at the time.

Although **St Joseph's Crescent**, off Christian Street, was named after a local church, it is co-incidentally apt that St. Joseph is the patron saint of workers. His feast day is 1st May and was selected as a counter celebration to the Soviet Union's May Day celebrations. Also off Christian Street is **Tom Mann Close**, named after the co-founder of the Workers Union, which eventually merged with others to form the Trade & General Workers Union. In 1911 he led the transport workers strike in Liverpool and consequently served six months in jail for sedition. In Vauxhall, **Tolpuddle Way** is named after the Tolpuddle Martyrs, six farm labourers who were sentenced to transportation to Australia in 1834 after asking for a rise in wages. After a public outrage they were pardoned two years later and their struggle was a landmark in trade union history, with the right to 'free collective bargaining' being established.

Also in Vauxhall, two Irish political activists are commemorated. Back Bond Street disappeared and **O'Connell Road** was developed, named after early 19th century Irish political rights leader Daniel O'Connell. Another Irish Nationalist, James Larkin is commemorated by **James Larkin Way** in Kirkdale. He played a part in the 1916 Easter Rebellion. Next to James Larkin Way is **Sharpeville Close**, which commemorates the Sharpeville massacre of 1960 when sixty people were killed as South African police opened fire on a crowd of Black protesters.

Three new streets off Upper Stanhope Street in Toxteth reflect Liverpool's support for Nicaragua's left wing Sandinista government during this period. **Corinto Street** is named after the country's Pacific port with which very close ties were developed, while **Bluefields Street** is named after a Nicaraguan port on the Caribbean coast. **Sandino Street** commemorates Augusto Cesar Sandino, the 1920's guerrilla leader from whom the rebel group took its name when it was formed in the 1960s.

20TH CENTURY PRIVATE DEVELOPMENTS

W HILE MANY STREETS developed by the council were often named after places, private developers have sometimes been more imaginative in the naming of streets in Liverpool. However, when stuck, they have often reverted to the more simple method too.

When old streets near Heyworth Street and Breck Road in Everton that had been named after Everton were cleared and more modern housing built in their place, the new road names were derived from the old streets. **Landseer Road** is named after Sir Edwin Henry Landseer, who painted animals but is perhaps best known for sculpting the lions in Trafalgar Square. **Eastlake Avenue** remembers Sir Charles Lock Eastlake, who painted portraits and biblical scenes in the early 19th century. **Elmore Close** takes its name from Alfred Elmore, who painted historical scenes in Victorian times, most famously *The Martyrdom of Thomas à Becket*. Marine painter Clarkson Frederick Stanfield gives his name to **Stanfield Avenue**, while landscape painter Francis Danby is honoured by **Danby Close**.

In Stoneycroft, classical architectural styles were remembered in the 1920s. **Doric Road**, **Ionic Road** and **Corinthian Avenue** are named after the three different types of Greek architectural column, while their decorative features are remembered by **Abacus Road** and **Acanthus Road**. The Etruscan civilisation, who lived on the Italian peninsula before the Roman Empire have given their name to **Etruscan Road**, while **Podium Road** takes its name from the base on which Etruscan temples would stand. **Classic Road** is named after the classical forms of architecture, which the Greeks and Romans adapted. This was revived in the Renaissance of the 15th and 16th centuries by Italian architects including Andrea Palladio, who has been commemorated in **Palladio Road**. **Florentine Road** remembers the architects of Florence who contributed to this renaissance, while **Inigo Road** is named after Inigo Jones, an English architect of the 17th century who was inspired by Palladio. More architects are remembered in off Utting Avenue Anfield by **Vanbrugh Road, Vanbrugh Crescent, Hildebrand Road** and **Hildebrand Crescent**, named after Sir John

Vanbrugh, who designed Blenheim Palace and Johann Lukas Von Hildebrandt, who designed a number of palaces in Vienna.

Liverpool's famous river is the Mersey, but its little sister, the Alt, has not been forgotten. In Croxteth Park, perhaps the city's most famous street, **Brookside**, set for the Channel 4 soap opera that ran from 1982 to 2003 and restored to housing in 2011, takes its name from it due to the rivers proximity. On the same estate there is a **Riverside**, with **Bridge Gardens** situated next to where Deysbrook Lane goes over it. River features give their names to **Delta Drive, Oxbow Road, The Dell** and **The Meander**. Staying in Croxteth but nearer to the East Lancashire Road, **Altcross Road** and **Altcross Way** are named in relation to the former including a bridge over the river.

Another water feature, now disused is the Kensington Reservoir. This has given its name to **Clearwater Close**. Off Smithdown Road in Wavertree, there is a **Brookdale Road**. This is named after the Upper Brook stream, that used to flow down Smithdown Road and into Greenbank Park nearby. In Kirkdale, a number of streets named after rivers were demolished and new housing built, but with the new closes developed taking the names of what was there earlier. They are **Avon Close**, **Doon Close**, **Humber Close** and **Tyne Close**.

For a city so steeped in football heritage, the sport is virtually forgotten about in the local street names and is only commemorated in two places. **Mere Green** in Walton takes its name from the original name for Everton FC's Goodison Park ground. **Bob Paisley Court**, a sheltered block, is situated barely a goal kick away from the Kop end at Anfield and remembers Liverpool FC managerial legend Bob Paisley.

Liverpool's famous horse race, the Grand National is well represented by local street names, with estates bordering Aintree racecourse along its lines. Streets present include **Red Rum Close**, named after the three times seventies winner, while **Eremon Close**, **Sunloch Close**, **Sprig Close, Kilmore Close, Anglo Close** and **Papillon Drive** are named after the winners of 1907, 1914, 1927, 1962 and 1966 and 2000. Other streets on this estate linked to the race are **Seagram Close**, after a former sponsor and **Foxhunter Drive**, after the Foxhunter Chase that is run on the first day of the Grand National meeting and open to amateur riders. **Furlong Close** is named after a horse racing term of distance, **Steeplechase Close**, refers to the fact the Grand National is run over jumps, **Hedgebank Close** is after a feature of a racecourse and **Saddle Close** is what riders use to sit on the horse. **Canter Close** is named after a term of horses movement. Maintaining the horse racing theme in this area is **Dante Close**, named after the Dante Stakes which is run at York every May and is a trial race for the Epsom Derby. In nearby Warbreck Park, **Woodbrook Avenue**, **Foinavon Close**, **Sundew Close**, **Lucius Close** and **Ayala Close** are all named after past winners of the race, whilst **Bechers Row** commemorates Aintree's most famous jump, Bechers Brook.

A number of famous golf courses give their names to streets locally too. Off Yew Tree Lane in West Derby, opposite the golf course are a number of streets named after other courses. The main road on the estate is **St. Andrews Avenue**, named after the famous Scottish course, which was the venue for the 2000 Open. Other Scottish courses are commemorated in **Carnoustie Close**, **Muirfield Close**, **Troon Close** and **Turnberry Close**, while **Belfry Close**, **Fulford Close**, **Rye Grove** and **Lytham Close** are named after English courses. Off Townsend Lane, **Birkdale Close** was built around the time of the 1984 Open, which was held at Birkdale, near Southport. The summer sport of cricket has been remembered by **Willow Way** and **Wicket Close** in Gillmoss, willow being the wood of which bats are made.

This is not to say private developers have not resorted to place names too however. One example is off Childwall Valley Road, where a number of towns and villages in the southwest are honoured. Examples are **Okehampton Road**, **Padstow Road** and **Paignton Road**. Not too far away off Childwall Park Avenue the southwest is honoured again, with **Devon Gardens**, **Woolacombe Road** and **Churston Road**. In Stoneycroft, not far from where Tynwald Hill was developed in the 19th century, the UK islands theme moves on to the Channel Islands, with **Guernsey Road** and **Sark Road**. Surprisingly there is no Jersey Road, but **Brelade Road** and **Portelet Road** are named after two of the islands popular bay areas.

Moving further away, there are small pockets of streets named from places around the world in different parts of Liverpool. In Fazakerley **Cape Road, Natal Road** and **Pretoria Road** are named after places in South Africa, with **Rhodesia Road** coming from the former name for Zimbabwe. Fazakerley also has some streets with an American connection, off Longmoor Lane streets are named in sequence with **First Avenue, Second Avenue, Third Avenue, Fourth Avenue, Fifth Avenue, Sixth Avenue** and **Seventh Avenue**, a pattern first adopted by many American cities. In Tuebrook, American states have given their name to **California Road, Missouri Road** and **Pennsylvania Road**. Another American themed street is **Tupelo Close** in Croxteth, after Tupelo in Mississippi, birthplace of Elvis Presley.

In Woolton, where a school was operating in the 17th century, there are five streets named after educational establishments. **Charterhouse Road** is named after Charterhouse School in Surrey, one of the elite group of public schools in the country. **Haileybury Road** takes its name from Haileybury & Imperial Service College in Hertfordshire, which has the largest academic quadrangle in the world. Roedean, an independent girls school in Sussex that has a sister school in South Africa gives its name to **Roedean Close**. Beatles manager Brian Epstein's old school Wrekin College is remembered by **Wrekin Close** and **Stonyhurst Road** is named after Stonyhurst College in Lancashire, which continues to adhere to the Jesuit tradtion.

School Lane in Woolton eventually leads to Hunts Cross, where there is another group of school streets, again with a Beatles connection. Stowe School in Buckingham, after which **Stowe Close** is named, was the venue for a concert by the band in 1963. They had accepted an invitation by boarder David Moores, who would go on to become chairman of Liverpool FC. 450 year old Oundle School in Northamptonshire gives rise to **Oundle Place,** while **Winchester Close** is named after Winchester College, which was founded in 1382 and claims to be the oldest public school in the country.

At the end of the 1990s one development off East Prescot Road had an astrological theme, with the developer naming streets as it was a case of new beginnings for those moving there. The estate comprises **Taurus Road, Aquarius Close, Capricorn Crescent, Leo Close, Aries Close, Scorpio Close** and **Libra Close**.

Liverpool's most famous sons are the Beatles. In the 1980s **George Harrison Close, John Lennon Drive, Paul McCartney Way** and **Ringo Starr Drive** were all named after them in Kensington. It was proposed around the turn of the millennium that North John Street be renamed John Street, or even John Lennon Street, a topic that sparked fierce debate.

When Wavertree Technology Park was developed towards the end of the 1980s, the theme of the new roads laid out was scientists. **Faraday Road** remembers Michael Faraday who discovered the laws of electrolysis and **Newton Court** is named after Sir Isaac Newton who defined the law of universal gravitation. Ernest Rutherford, a pioneering name in nuclear physics, gives his name to **Rutherford Close**. The second phase of the park, nearer the railway line saw **Stephenson Way**, named after George Stephenson who designed the Rocket train that ran on the Liverpool & Manchester railway when it opened in 1830. Stephenson lived in Tapton House in Chesterfield, after which **Tapton Way** is named. The house is now part of Chesterfield College.

After the closure of the Standard Triumph motor works in Hunts Cross in the early 1980s, a trading park has been developed. The main road through it is **Triumph Way**, whilst models of cars have been remembered by **Dolomite Avenue**, **Herald Avenue**, **Mayflower Avenue**, **Spitfire Road** and **Vitesse Road**

One of the greatest success stories nationally in the 1980s was the building of the Eldonian Village. Local residents of tenements in the area refused to accept council proposals to break their community up and fought for the right to build homes on the site of the former Tate & Lyle factory. A housing co-operative was formed and the first residents moved into their new homes in 1989. The scheme went on to win a World Habitat Award from the United Nations. **Michael Dragonette Court** was named after one of the residents who played a key role in pushing the scheme in the early days, working voluntarily in their Eldon Street office, but died before its completion. His daughter Margaret continues to work for what is now a community based housing association. Harry Burrows, after whom **Burrows Court** was named, was another resident involved at the beginning, as was Billy Little from the Portland Gardens Co-operative, who trained in horticulture at the age of 60 and went on to work in the Eldonian Garden Market. **Little Court** is named after him. Tom Fleming, a well known member of the local community who was a teacher in Our Lady's school in Eldon Street was honoured by **Fleming Court**.

Two other streets on the Eldonian Village are named after housing officials. Max Steinberg, after whom **Max Steinberg Court** is named was a Housing Corporation official who saw the benefits of the scheme and worked tirelessly to convince government officials it was sustainable. He is now Chief Executive of regeneration company Liverpool Vision. **Jack McBane Court** is named after a local housing manager who helped get the scheme off the ground. He has since worked in regeneration around the country and in 2008 published the book *"The Rebirth of Liverpool – The Eldonian Way"*. Head of the Mersey Docks and Harbour Company where many of the residents worked at the time, Jim Fitzpatrick, gave his name to **Fitzpatrick Court**. He oversaw massive changes at the port in this period but did so in a caring manner, arranging loans with central government so that all of the 75% of the workforce who had to leave did so by voluntary means with enhanced redundancy packages. Jim took a place on the Eldonian Development Trust, now the Eldonian Board and died in 2006.

INTO THE 21ST CENTURY

MANY OF THE NEW STREETS that have appeared in the 21st century have already been covered in other chapters. However there are some that don't necessarily fit into any category and as such are being put together here.

The Liverpool One development saw a number of streets disappear or be re-aligned and new ones emerge, with the new names given reflecting the heritage of the area, some of which were reincarnations of previous ones. However a new name altogether was **Wall Street,** as it runs roughly along the old walls of Liverpool Castle. It also demonstrates Liverpool's American connection, Wall Street being a famous financial centre in New York City.

Between Farnworth Street and Upper Baker Street in Kensington, re-alignment of older properties and new developments has led to the creation of **Olympia Street**, after the nearby Olympia Theatre. Built in 1905 as a variety and circus venue, it could accommodate 3750 but after the 2nd World War it was renamed the Locarno and became a bingo and nightclub venue. In the late 1990s it re-opened as a theatre and has been used for concerts and boxing due to its central stage, with a capacity of up to 1,960

In Edge Hill, **Crown Station Place** has been developed and named after its proximity to the site of Crown Street Station, which was the original terminus of the Liverpool and Manchester Railway. The growth of the railway meant that in 1836 the line was extended and Lime Street station built, making the station redundant after just six years.

New developments in Garston have retained connections with the areas past. **Cornfields Close** remembers a time when corn was grown in the locality before the area became urbanised in the early 20th century, the first mills having been established in the 13th century. At that time Adam de Gerstan was the landowner and he is commemorated by **Adam Close**. The same has happened in Childwall, where **Jacksons Pond Drive** is named after Jacksons Pond, which was situated nearby at what is now the Alderman John Village Gardens on Gateacre Park Drive.

The development of the Liverpool Innovation Park, an office and business space location off Edge Lane, has seen the creation of **Innovation Boulevard** and **Digital Way,** which reflects the availability of high tech digital technology.

Some new roads have simply reflected their surroundings, such as **Viewpark Close** in Childwall as it adjoins playing fields and **Railbrook Hey** in Wavertree as it is situated next to a railway line. Perhaps one of the more unusual clusters of new roads is off Childwall Valley Road, where there is a **Maderia Drive, Genoa Close, Simnel Close** and **Viennese Road**. The first edition of this book speculated on the cover introduction 'was Battenberg Street named after a cake'. The answer was no, but in these cases it is definitely yes.

In Anfield, a development by Keepmoat Homes and Arena Housing has seen roads named after species of plants that inhabit local parks – **Burnet Road, Reedmace Road** and **Tilia Road**, whilst the main road through the development, **Kemp Avenue**, remembers landscape architect Edward Kemp who designed Newsham Park, Stanley Park and Anfield Cemetery.

In 2011 the New Liverpool Beatles Appreciation Society suggested that others linked to the Beatles have streets named after them. They recommended drummer Pete Best, who was forced out of the group in 1962 to make way for Ringo Starr, Stuart Sutcliffe who left the group in 1961 to pursue a career as an artist but tragically died of an aneurism just nine months later, and manager Brian Epstein also be honoured. The council was amenable to the idea but said that no existing streets would be re-named, only ones in new developments could be considered. It was confirmed in July 2011 that two new streets on the Bellefield development in West Derby on the site of Everton FC's former training ground would be named **Pete Best Drive** and **Casbah Close**. The latter was after The Casbah, a café opened by Best's mother in nearby Haymans Green in 1959 where youngsters could go and listen to bands, the Beatles going on to be one of them.

Off Stonebridge Lane near the Gillmoss Industrial Estate the Devon and Cornwall theme from other side of East Lancashire Road has continued. **Longdown Road, Carbis Close, Carland Close, Fistral Close, Pentire Close** and **Travanson Close** are all named after places in the south west counties. Another area where an earlier development continued was with **October Drive** in Tuebrook. This carried on a theme of roads named after months of the year that had been developed over a hundred years earlier. It has been suggested that only months between March and September were initially named as others seemed too grim. In this case it seems the developer has added just one more and other roads in the new development haven't extended to the darkest winter months.

Finally, Scousers have always been known for their sense of humour and there has been an ironic development in Dovecot on the site of the old East Prescot Road baths. The site is opposite a Mecca bingo hall but the new street is named **Gala Close**, in relation to the swimming galas that would have taken place there. However it is also the name of a rival bingo company, meaning it may either have been named by a developer with a wicked sense of humour, or has turned out to be just an unfortunate coincidence...

INDEX

Brook Street   27
Brougham Terrace   64
Brownlow Hill   32
Brownlow Street   32
Brunswick Road   68
Brunswick Street   68
Brunswick Way   69
Brydges Street   76
Buckingham Road (L9 & L13)   70
Burlington Street   64
Burnage Close   113
Burnet Road   124
Burrows Court   121
Bute Street   61
Buttercup Way   86
Byrom Street   33
Byron Street   105
Cadet Way   84
Cadogan Street 60
Cairnmore Road   90
Cairns Street 64
Caithness Road   90
Caledonia Street   89
California Road   120
Callaghan Close   66
Calmet Close   99
Cambridge Street   68
Campania Street   44
Campbell Street   30
Canada Boulevard   83
Canalside Grove   42
Canberra Lane   84
Canning Place   57
Canning Street   57
Canon Road   99
Canterbury Street   100
Canter Close   119
Cape Road   119
Capricorn Crescent   120
Capstick Crescent   115
Carbis Close   124
Cardigan Way   89
Cardiff Way   89
Carland Close   124
Carnatic Road   54
Carnegie Road   37
Carnoustie Close   119
Caronia Street   44

Carpathia Street   44
Carpenters Row   42
Carstairs Road   89
Carrickmore Avenue   90
Carver Street   14
Caryl Street   15
Casbah Close   124
Cases Street 29
Caspian Road   114
Castlefield Road   6
Castlesite Road   6
Castle Street   3
Castletown Close   45
Castlewood Road   108
Catharine Street   88
Cathedral Road   99
Cavan Road   81
Cavell Close   83
Cavendish Drive   64
Cecil Street   59
Celia Street   105
Celt Street   89
Celtic Street   107
Central Avenue   113
Central Way   113
Chadwick Street   32
Chapel Road   99
Chapel Street   4
Charles Berrington Road   100
Charleston Road   79
Charterhouse Road   120
Chase Way   39
Chatham Street   61
Chatsworth Drive   65
Chaucer Street   103
Cheapside   23
Chedworth Road   114
Chelsea Road   70
Chelwood Avenue   60
Cherry Lane   6
Chesterfield Street   15
Cheviot Road   89
Childers Street   65
Childwall Abbey Road 6
Childwall Avenue   60
Childwall Priory Road   6
Christian Street   32
Christopher Close   100

Christopher Way   100
Church Alley   91
Church Avenue   92
Churchfield Road   96
Church Road L15   95
Church Road L25   95
Church Road North   95
Church Road South   95
Church Street   91
Churchill Way   66
Churston Road   119
Clamley Road   113
Claremont Road   70
Clarence Street   68
Clarendon Road   64
Classic Road   117
Clay Cross Road   53
Claypole Close   106
Clayton Square   29
Clearwater Close   118
Cleveland Square   28
Cleveley Park   55
Cleveley Road   55
Clough Road   113
Clwyd Grove   89
Clyde Road   89
Coachmans Drive   16
Coal Street   32
Coburg Wharf   69
Cockburn Street   77
Cockshead Road   115
Cockspur Street   28
Coleridge Street   65
College Lane   29
Colombus Quay   43
Colonel Drive   84
Columbus Quay   43
Colquitt Street   30
Colwell Road   114
Comus Street   103
Coningsby Road   108
Coniston Street   48
Conleach Road   111
Connaught Road   71
Conwy Drive   89
Cooper Avenue North   38
Cooper Avenue South   38
Copperas Hill   32

Copperfield Close   106
Cornfields Close   123
Corinthian Avenue   117
Corinto Street   115
Cornfields Street   123
Cornwallis Street   78
Costain Street   90
Cottenham Street   65
Cotton Street   42
Coventry Road   100
Crabtree Close   114
Cranbourne Road   60
Cranmer Street   97
Craven Lea   16
Crawford Avenue   74
Crawford Drive   51
Creswell Street   58
Critchley Road   112
Crocus Street   86
Crompton's Lane   52
Cromwell Street   73
Crosshall Street   10
Crossley Drive   52
Crossways   6
Crow Street   20
Crown Station Place   123
Croxdale Road   114
Croxteth Drive   16
Croxteth Grove   16
Croxteth Hall Lane   16
Croxteth Road   16
Cullen Street   106
Culme Road   81
Cumberland Street   67
Cunliffe Street   18
Curate Road   99
Custom House Place   31
Dahlia Close   86
Dale Street   3
Dalrymple Street   33
Damwood Road   113
Danby Close   117
Dane Street   88
Dansie Street   32
Dante Close   119
Daulby Street   22
Davidson Road   82
David Street   97

Deacon Court   96
Dean Dillistone Court   96
Deane Road   31
Dean Patey Court   96
Delagoa Road   81
Delta Drive   118
Denbigh Street   87
Denman Drive   65
Denman Road   65
Denman Street   65
Deptford Close   114
Derby Road   14
Derby Square   13
Devon Gardens   119
Devonshire Road   65
Devonshire Road West   65
Dickens Street   106
Digital Way   124
Dingle Vale   21
Dinorwic Road   88
Doddridge Street   97
Dolomite Avenue   121
Dombey Street   106
Dominic Close   100
Dominic Road   100
Doon Close   118
Dorans Lane   30
Doric Road   117
Dorien Road   82
Dorrit Street   106
Douglas Close   50
Douro Street   78
Dovecot Avenue   50
Dovecot Place   50
Dover Grove   45
Dovey Street   87
Dowesfield Lane   54
Downing Street   62
Druids Cross Gardens   53
Druids Cross Road   53
Druids Park   53
Druidsville Road   53
Drury Lane   24
Dryden Street   104
Dublin Street   44
Dudlow Drive   52
Dudlow Gardens   52
Dudlow Lane   52

Dudlow Nook Road   52
Duke Street   67
Dunbar Street   73
Duncan Street   76
Dunkeld Street   89
Dunmore Road   89
Dunnerdale Road   114
Durham Street   100
Durning Road   37
Durrington Brook   114
Dymchurch Road   114
Dyson Street   88
Earle Road   19
Earle Street   19
Easby Road   99
East Albert Road   70
Eastbourne Road   71
Eastdale Road   51
East Damwood Road   113
Eastern Avenue   113
Eastlake Avenue   117
East Millwood Road   113
Eberle Street   35
Edgewell Drive   5
Edith Road   88
Edmund Street   10
Elaine Street   107
Eldon Grove   63
Eldon Place   63
Eldon Street   63
Ellel Grove   36
Ellerman Road   43
Elliot Street   76
Elm Close   86
Elm Hall Drive   55
Elmore Close   117
Elmsfield Close   53
Elms House Road   50
Elmswood Road   54
Elmway   50
Elsie Road   88
Elton Street
Elwy Street   87
Emery Street   88
Empress Road (L6 & L7)   71
Enid Street   107
Eremon Close   118
Erskine Street   63

Grace Road   99
Grace Street   97
Grafton Street   61
Grampian Road   89
Grange Street   36
Grange Terrace   51
Granville Road   64
Grasmere Street   48
Grayson Street   42
Great Charlotte Street   68
Great Crosshall Street   11
Great George Place   68
Great George Square   68
Great George Street   68
Great Homer Street   103
Great Howard Street   62
Great Newton Street   18
Great Orford Street   18
Greenbank Drive   22
Greenbank Lane   22
Greenbank Road   22
Greenhill Road 54
Greenland Street   42
Greenleaf Street   106
Greenock Street   89
Greenough Street   53
Gregory Close   100
Gregory Way   100
Gregson Street   33
Grenville Street South   63
Greyhound Farm Road   112
Grovehurst Avenue
Grove Street   85
Guelph Street   71
Guernsey Road   119
Gwendoline Street   107
Gwent Close   89
Gwydir Street   87
Hackins Hey   9
Hadassah Grove 97
Haileybury Road   120
Hale Road   112
Halkirk Road   90
Hall Lane   49
Halsbury Road   65
Halsey Avenue   81
Halsey Crescent   81
Hampden Street   73

Hanover Street   67
Hardinge Road   64
Hardman Street   57
Hardy Street   77
Harefield Green   113
Harefield Road   113
Harland Green   112
Harper Street   33
Harrington Road   43
Harrismith Road   81
Harrison Way   43
Harrowby Close   58
Harrowby Street   58
Harthill Avenue   53
Harthill Road   53
Hartington Road   64
Hartley Quay   41
Harwich Grove   45
Hatton Garden   33
Hawdon Court   106
Hawke Street   75
Heathcote Road   93
Heathfield Road   51
Heathgate Avenue   112
Heaton Close   113
Hector Place   105
Hedgebank Close   119
Helena Street (L7 & L9)   71
Herald Avenue   121
Herculaneum Court   79
Herculaneum Road   79
Hereford Road   100
Hermes Road   84
Herschell Street 63
Hewitson Avenue   81
Hewitson Road   81
High Street   3
High Street (Wavertree)   5
High Street (Woolton)   6
Hildebrand Close   117
Hildebrand Road   117
Hilltop Road   52
Hockenhall Alley   9
Holland Road   112
Hollins Close   52
Holly Farm Road   6
Holmefield Road   54
Holme Street   36

Lascelles Road   72
Latham Street   14
Lathbury Lane   16
Latimer Street   98
Laurel Road   85
Lavan Close   88
Lavan Street   88
Lavender Way   86
Lawrence Road   33
Leather Lane   28
Lee Hall Road   52
Leeds Street   42
Leigh Street   29
Leinster Road   44
Lenham Way   114
Lenthall Street   73
Leo Close   120
Lester Close   93
Leopold Road   71
Leveret Road   113
Libra Close   120
Lichfield Road   100
Liddell Road   82
Lightbody Street   33
Lightwood Drive   106
Lilley Road   85
Lilian Road   88
Limekiln Lane   32
Lime Street   32
Limetree Close   86
Lincoln Street   100
Lindisfarne Drive   101
Lind Street   88
Linner Road   112
Linton Street   88
Lisburn Lane   48
Lismore Road   90
Liston Street   88
Little Court   121
Littledale   34
Little Heath Road   113
Little Woolton Street   19
Livingston Drive North   86
Livingston Drive South   86
Llanwryst Close   87
Lochinvar Street   104
Lochmore Road   90
Lockfields View   42

Lodge Lane   16
Lomond Road   89
London Road   23
Longdown Road   124
Longfellow Street   107
Lord Nelson Street   77
Lord Street   15
Lorne Street   89
Lothair Road   108
Lovel Road   112
Lovel Way   112
Lowell Street   88
Lowerson Road   82
Lucania Street   44
Lucius Close   119
Lusitania Road   44
Lunsford Road   114
Lutyens Close   91
Lydia Ann Street   79
Lynsted Road   114
Lytham Close   119
Macbeth Street   105
Macdonald Street   80
Maddocks Street   94
Madeira Drive   124
Madryn Street   87
Magdala Street   81
Major Street   93
Makin Street   88
Mandeville Street   73
Manica Crescent   83
Mannering Road   104
Mansfield Street   77
Marlborough Road   70
Marlborough Street   74
Marlowe Close   105
Marmion Road   104
Marybone   92
Maryland Street   31
Masefield Grove   109
Mason Street   33
Mather Avenue   38
Mathew Street   41
Maud Street   107
Mauretania Road   44
Max Steinberg Court   121
Maxwell Road   82
Mayflower Avenue   121

Olive Mount Road   52
Olive Mount Walk   52
Olney Street   88
Olympia Street   123
O'Reilly Court   94
Orient Drive   53
Origen Road   101
Ormond Street   75
Orphan Drive   86
Orthes Street   78
Osborne Road   70
Othello Close   105
Otway Street   105
Oundle Place   120
Out Lane   6
Overbury Street   108
Overton Street   108
Oxbow Road   118
Oxford Street   24
Oxton Street   88
Paddington   25
Padstow Road   119
Paignton Road   119
Paisley Street   89
Palace Road   71
Palladio Road   117
Pall Mall   23
Palmerston Road   64
Papillon Drive   118
Paradise Street   41
Parker Street   29
Parliament Street   15
Parr Street   30
Patmos Close   104
Paul McCartney Way   120
Paul Orr Court   39
Peach Street   85
Peacehaven Close   45
Pearson Street   51
Pecksniff Street   106
Peel Street   64
Pendennis Street   108
Pengwern Street   87
Pennsylvania Road   120
Penny Lane   19
Penrhyn Street   57
Pentire Road   124
Penuel Road   93

Perth Street   89
Pete Best Drive   124
Peterborough Road   100
Peters Lane   91
Petherick Road   114
Petra Close   40
Peveril Street   104
Phillimore Road   65
Pickop Street   33
Pickwick Street   106
Picton Crescent   37
Picton Grove   37
Picton Road   37
Pitt Street   61
Pitville Avenue   54
Pitville Road   54
Plumer Street   80
Plumpton Street   33
Podium Road   117
Portelet Road   119
Porter Street   32
Portia Street   105
Portland Street   63
Powis Street   87
Pownall Square   28
Pownall Street   28
Premier Street   62
Prenton Green   113
Prescot Road   7
Preston Grove   36
Pretoria Road   119
Price Street   28
Prince Albert Mews   69
Prince Alfred Road   69
Princes Avenue   69
Princes Road   69
Prince William Street   68
Priors Close   95
Priorsfield Road   95
Priory Street   95
Priory Way   95
Prussia Street   75
Pudsey Street   32
Pugin Street   91
Pym Street   73
Quakers Alley   92
Quarry Street   53
Queen Anne Street   67

St Marys Street   95
St Nicholas Place   92
St Oswalds Street   94
St Paschal Baylon Boulevard   96
St Stephens Close   96
St Stephens Place   92
St Vincent Street   76
St Vincent Way   76
Saddle Close   119
Salisbury Road 59
Salthouse Quay   18
Sandino Steet   116
Sandon Street   58
Sandon Way 58
Sandown Lane   51
Sandown Road   51
Sandringham Drive   70
Sandringham Road   70
Sankey Street   41
Sark Road   119
Saxonia Road   44
Saxony Road   71
Scargreen Avenue   114
Scarisbrick Crescent   49
Scarisbrick Drive   49
Scarisbrick Place   49
Scarisbrick Road   49
Schomberg Street   74
School Lane   11
School Way   112
Score Lane   6
Scorpio Close   120
Scott Close   91
Seacole Close   79
Seagram Close   118
Seafarers Way   53
Second Avenue   120
Sedley Street   108
Seddon Road   59
Sedgemoor Road   74
Seel Street   30
Sefton Park Road   16
Sefton Road   16
Sefton Street   15
Selkirk Road   89
Seventh Avenue   120
Shakespeare Close   105
Shakespeare Street   105

Shand Street   38
Sharpeville Close   115
Sheil Road   36
Shelley Grove   105
Shenstone Street   108
Sheridan Street   104
Sidney Place   108
Silvester Street 94
Simnel Close   124
Sir Howard Street   58
Sir Howard Way   58
Sir Thomas Street   57
Sixth Avenue   120
Skerries Road   88
Skirving Street   62
Slater Place   75
Slater Street   75
Sleepers Hill   5
Sheridan Street   103
Snowdrop Street   86
Soho Street   25
Solomon Street   49
Somerford Road   114
South Albert Road   70
Southdale Road 51
Southern Road   113
South Hunter Street   31
South John Street   30
South Parade   113
South Sudley Road   54
Sparling Street   42
Sparrow Hall Road   4
Speke Church Road   112
Spekelands Road   19
Speke Town Lane   112
Spellow Lane   49
Spellow Place   27
Spencer Street   41
Spitfire Road   121
Sprig Close   118
Springbank Road   47
Springwood Avenue   55
Spurgeon Close   99
Stainburn Avenue   114
Stamfordham Drive   72
Standale Road   51
Stand Park Road   52
Stanfield Avenue   117

Ulster Road   44
Ultonia Street   44
Ulverston Close   114
Umbria Street   44
Union Street   10
Upper Frederick Street   67
Upper Pitt Street   61
Upper Pownall Street   28
Upper Harrington Street   15
Upper Stanhope Street   15
Upper Warwick Street   15
Upper William Street   69
Upton Close   113
Upton Green   113
Utting Avenue   38
Utting Avenue East   38
Valencia Road   51
Valley Road   88
Vanbrugh Crescent   117
Vanbrugh Road   117
Vandries Street   32
Vandyke Street   107
Vauxhall Road   23
Verdala Towers   54
Verona Street   105
Vicarage Lawn   96
Vicar Road   99
Victoria Avenue   69
Victoria Drive   70
Victoria Park   69
Victoria Road   70
Victoria Street   69
Victoria Terrace   69
Viennese Road   124
Viewpark Close   124
Village Street   5
Vitesse Road   121
Voelas Street   87
Vrynwy Street   88
Wall Street   123
Walmsley Street   35
Walnut Street   85
Walsingham Road   101
Walton Breck Road   48
Walton Hall Avenue   20
Walton Village   6
Wapping   24
Wapshare Road   81

Warwick Street   15
Waterhouse Street   47
Waterloo Quay   78
Waterloo Road   77
Waterloo Street   78
Water Street   4
Wauchope Street   80
Waverley Road   104
Weldon Street   88
Weller Street   106
Wellesley Road   78
Wellesley Terrace   78
Wellington Road   78
Wellington Street L8 78
Wellington Street L19 64
Well Lane   6
Wellstead Road 5
Wendell Street   106
Wesley Place   95
West Albert Road   70
Westdale Road   51
Western Avenue   113
West Oakhill Park 50
Westminster Road   98
Whitechapel   23
Whiteside Close   94
Whitley Street   59
Whittier Street   106
Wicket Close   119
Wilbraham Street   14
Wilburn Street   88
Wilfer Close   106
William Brown Street   59
William Henry Street   69
William Jessop Way   42
William Moult Street   14
Williamson Square   29
Williamson Street   29
Willow Way   119
Winchester Close   120
Windermere Street   48
Windsor Road (L13 & L9)   70
Winkle Street   106
Winslow Street   88
Winstone Road   114
Withington Road   113
Wolfe Street   75
Woodbrook Avenue   119